THE TRUE VORTICES

A JOURNEY THROUGH THE CHAKRAS

SATHYAJITH DIVAKARAN NAIR

Copyright © Sathyajith Divakaran Nair
All Rights Reserved.

This book has been published with all efforts taken to make the material error-free after the consent of the author. However, the author and the publisher do not assume and hereby disclaim any liability to any party for any loss, damage, or disruption caused by errors or omissions, whether such errors or omissions result from negligence, accident, or any other cause.

While every effort has been made to avoid any mistake or omission, this publication is being sold on the condition and understanding that neither the author nor the publishers or printers would be liable in any manner to any person by reason of any mistake or omission in this publication or for any action taken or omitted to be taken or advice rendered or accepted on the basis of this work. For any defect in printing or binding the publishers will be liable only to replace the defective copy by another copy of this work then available.

To the Divine within me, that is the Divine within U...

Contents

Foreword

The many-hued chakras are our rainbow bridge to freedom. We are all born with this wisdom, it is our original template for transformation. If we are fortunate, we get to unveil the mystery that is actually so intimate to us. The chakras define who we are.

The first time I heard about the Chakra System, I was in utter amazement. It felt as if, having being lost in a dense forest for a long time, finally a path was lit up! In my naivete, I thought that all I now had to do was to get them up and running in a perfect way. Ah! Wait! I was yet to discover that they were teaching me putting my life in order, at all levels.

The one person who shared my excitement at the possibility this system presented for us, was my dear friend Sathyajit. Just like someone is a natural at music, or painting, or crunching numbers, Sathya (as we lovingly call him) is a natural at understanding the chakra system. He's intuitively tuned in, and can feel and sense them with great accuracy. I quickly found out that what he brings forth, comes from the fruit of his deep wisdom and experience, as he can unerringly guide you in these matters.

In this book, Sathya will take you on a step-by-step journey of evolution, and slowly open up the mystery. Inevitably, an inner alchemical transformation begins to happen on this voyage. My suggestion is not to rush through the book. Each chapter invites you to stay with a chakra, contemplate, and spend time diving into the mystery of each of them. The book is laid out like an experiential process. It works with light and shadow, feminine and masculine, spirit and matter, in the container of the body and the psyche. You will begin to see the chakras as gates that you pass through, to ever expanding states of consciousness. The passage from one chakra to the next, is an alchemical process, and if done with sincerity, there are great rewards.

When I began working with the chakras, I found that their unhealthy, blocked or stuck state was due the patterns I was stuck in, and the unhealthy and outdated belief systems and values I held. I began to take responsibility for having caused the block, and to clear it. This journey to consciousness began the process of truly becoming an adult. There is no other way to open the door, except through integrity. Deep conversations with Sathya, leading to many insights and aha moments, made this journey not just bearable, but enjoyable.

Sathya brings in a vast experience, having worked with hundreds of people individually and through his immensely popular workshops. By bringing out this book, he is touching the lives of so many people. I continue to learn and grow in his presence and wish him all the best on his journey.

Sukhvinder Sircar
Facilitator of Divine Feminine Workshops for Women and Men
Kolkata

Preface

This is an attempt to crystallize the Wisdom that Chose to come to me and is just an introduction of the same, a very simplified version, which hopefully can be easily understood.

My Conscious Spiritual journey began in the year 2009. It began with attending a Reiki session during which my Reiki master Shardamani Bhaskar, took me through a meditation of the chakras. For me it was an opening beyond what was told during the meditation. She just told me that the Mooladhara was red, and Abundance radiated out of it. I understood the connection between the Mother, Money, our patterns and the rest as a knowing that came from the Wisdom that poured out much beyond her words. Similarly for all the chakras.

However, at that point the Wisdom was rather diffuse. I did realise I got from her more than she realised or that the Universe was feeding me more stuff, however, all of it crystalized when I sat before my master Ranganatha Iyer for his 'Who am I' sessions. That is when all the Wisdom organised itself into clearly formed chakras and I understood how it all fell into place in the larger picture of the Universe. Again, not much of what is written here has been taught or told by him. He did much better. He opened the doors to Wisdom for me which was beyond him and directly from the Universe. For that I am eternally Grateful to him.

Both of them taught what was the most important to them and in turn opened up a stream of Wisdom which was independent of either.

Since then, I have been conducting workshops. In fact, this is where Sukhvinder Sircar comes in. She was also a follower of Ranganatha Iyer. It was she created the first two workshops for me and was my co-facilitator. She is a woman who made me realise the Goddess in every woman and every man and most importantly within me.

What has poured out through me was initially an extempore kind of workshop where I spoke about whatever was coming up and made sense. Later as my wife Manju Meenakshy and my soul mate Praveen Ghumnar joined me in this workshop series, we crystalized the curriculum to include all the basic things that are important and added activities that helped to make the curriculum easier to understand.

And then in 2020 I felt I had to write down at least some of the Wisdom so that it can be understood by a larger group of people.

And so, *the True Vortices* came into being...

Acknowledgements

Gratitude

My heart overflows with Gratitude to the following energies...

The Divine – For everything... Every single thing

My parents Divakaran Nair and Suseela Nair for playing the roles of my parents in this lifetime

My sister Suma Divakar for being by my side always

My master Ranganatha Iyer for guiding me to Oneness

My Reiki master, Sharda Mani Bhaskar for Reiki

My aunt Asha mami for introducing the concept of Kundalini to me even when I did not know what it was

My wife Manju Meenakshy – For her unstinted support, her Spiritual core, for reading the first draft and for her Love

My soul mate Praveen Ghumnar for being part of the True Vortices and taking so many sessions by my side

My dear friend Deepali Jain Ghumnar for always supporting us

My dear friend and Spiritual influencer Sukhvinder Sircar who is a fantastic mentor and guide, who took the time to read this book and write the foreward for me

My friend Farzana Bharmal for continuously prodding me to write this book

My friend Prarthana Patil, someone who has worked with me on the chakras, for reading the first draft and giving her feedback

My cousin Arathy Santhosh for painstakingly reading the first draft and giving her feedback as a total novice to chakras

And YOU!

CHAPTER ONE

The Sacred Anatomy

Welcome to this journey! I promise you; it will be worth it...

On this journey we will answer the important questions of our existence:

Why are we born?

Why do we suffer?

Is there a way I can control what happens to me?

Is eternal life real?

What is the Divine?

How am I connected to the Divine?

We will need to understand what our Sacred anatomy is to get to these answers. By 'Sacred anatomy' I mean the Divine anatomy which is more than just our body. We will get into the energy structures and understand what lies even beyond.

The body that we choose in a human lifetime has all the Sacred secrets that the Divine has so cleverly hidden in it.

Every curve, every scar, every colour has a secret to tell of its own that goes beyond the ordinary. The reason for the part being there... and the things we have added on to it which exhibits as pain, pleasure and more.

Let me explain.

I will restrict this explanation to the human species. There is a reason why we are the way we are with our feet on the ground, our hips atop our legs, our stomach above this, our heart placed where it is, why the throat is the thinnest part of the body, why our eyes only allow us binary vision and why there is an anterior fontanelle and a posterior fontanelle (the two almost cartilaginous areas in the skull that we can feel as soft spots on the skull in babies). Yes, this will be interesting for each one of you as the answers are very simple and will make sense to you too. But that will be discussed in detail through the book.

Some more broad parameters of the anatomy that we need to understand to understand why we exhibit pain and even fractures in parts of the body and why we even get dreadful diseases like cancer and diabetes.

We will be talking of the body as seen through the now universally accepted aspect as E = mc square or as the energy equation.

We will understand each of these points even better as we go through the "Chakras".

Ok, so what are chakras?

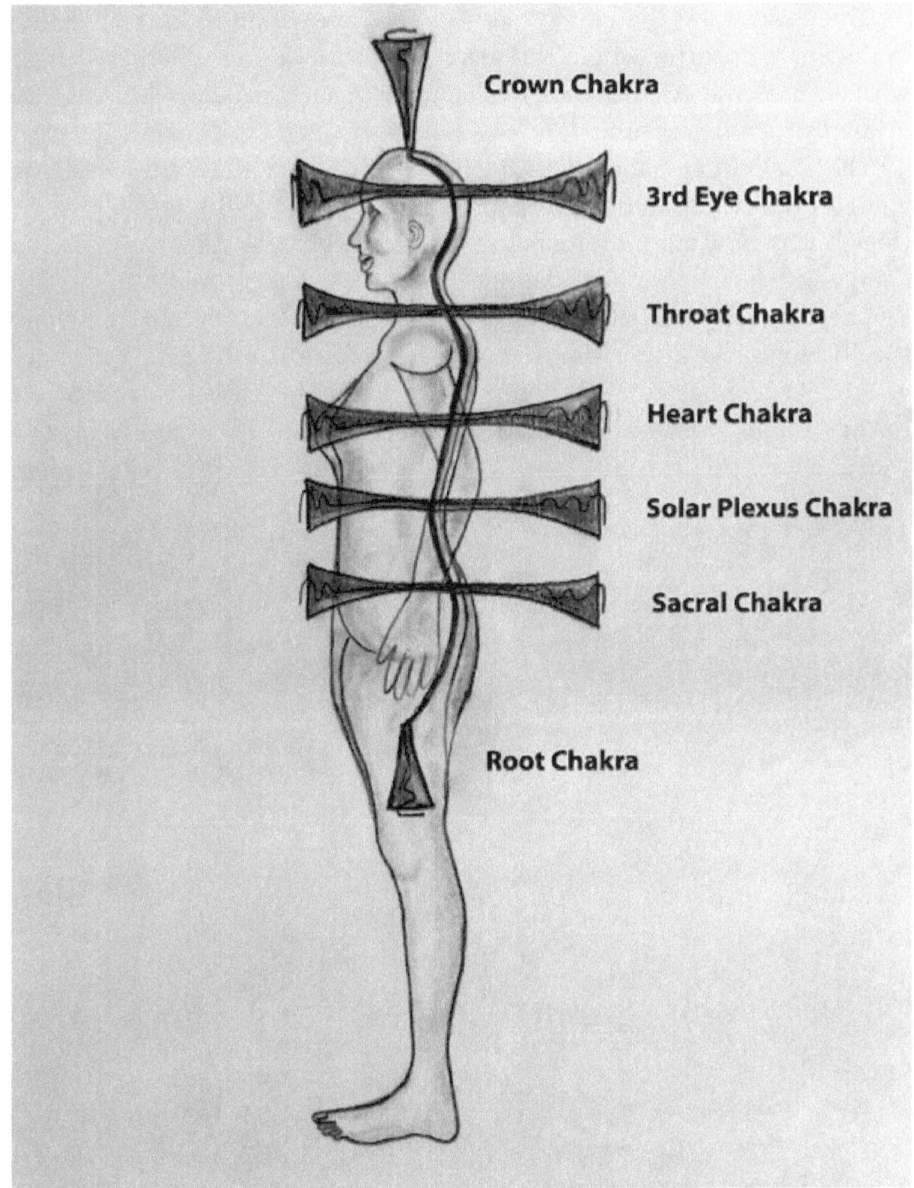

Fig 1: The seven important chakras and their positions in our body

Fig 1: The positions of the chakras along the spine in the human body with the crown chakra pointing towards the sky and the root chakra pointing towards

Mother Earth

The chakras are the energy vortices that are within us corresponding to the energy centres within this giant body that we call us that makes us what we are. And yes, there are over a hundred such chakras within us. But primarily there are seven.

The chakras are not physical phenomenon, but they are sensed as energies and their nature corresponds to the endocrine glands in our body, though it is of a more profound nature in the chakras. They are like the energy which controls the endocrine glands.

The major chakras are laid out as a straight line along our spine and specifically along a thin line right in the centre of the spine which we call the Sushumna nadi, thus forming a garland. This garland of chakras is further connected between two consecutive chakras by the fiery pingala nadi and the cold ida nadi.

Fig 2: The seven chakras when seen from the front of the body

Fig 2: The chakras along the body showing where each chakra is and their shapes

The chakras start from the base chakra (root chakra or Mooladhar chakra) located in the base of the spine and with a very high density and the further chakras are added on to the same above with each of them becoming lesser and lesser dense and consequently becoming faster and faster (as they are all spinning) and finally it becomes the most subtle energy of the Sahasraar chakra or the Crown chakra above the head which spins the fastest.

The chakras in order from the root Chakra are Mooladhar (yes, that's right, it is the root Chakra), followed by Swadhishtaan (Sacral) a few inches below the navel, after which comes the Manipura (Solar plexus) which is situated around the navel, the Anahata (Heart chakra) in the region of the Heart, the Vishuddhi (throat chakra), followed by the Ajna chakra (third eye) and finally the Sahasraar chakra.

There is one more detail I need to tell you. There are 3 knots or granthis in this garland with the first one just before the root chakra called the Brahma Granthi named after the creator God in Hinduism – Brahma. This is a constriction or knot in the energy flow which caused us to forget our true selves (we will understand this better in the Mooladhar) and causes us to believe that we are separate from the Divine. The second knot is the Vishnu Granthi that comes in between the Manipura and the Anahata chakras. This releases one of the misconceptions we live with – that of the presence of the 'other' in our lives. More of this later in the chapters between Swadhishtaan and Manipura. The third granthi is between the Vishuddhi and the Ajna chakras and is the final knot that clears the energy space making us realise our True nature – that we are the Divine.

So, picturise this – seven chakras spinning at their respective speeds with the root chakra forming one end of the garland of chakras or flowers and the Crown chakra forming the other end. Both these, the root chakra and the crown chakra has only one face with the root chakra facing downwards towards Mother Earth and the Crown chakra facing upwards towards Father Sky. The five chakras in between have two faces, one pointing inwards (into the body) and outwards (along the back of our body).

More details of the chakras will be in the subsequent chapters. Let's look at more peripheral details of the Sacred anatomy.

The body can be divided in two broad halves – The upper and the lower with the two halves joining at the region of the Heart.

The Lower portion pertains to all that is the mother or the 'Mother'. It includes both significations of our birth mother and our Divine Mother (Mother Earth or any other signification of the Divine Mother for that matter). And consequently, the upper portion is the 'Father' and includes all Spiritual essences of the 'Father God'.

In the sense of time, the body is again divisible into the past, the present and the future. From the lower part of the body to the upper, they are the past (feet up to the navel), the present (navel up to the throat) and the future (above the Throat).

The body is again divisible into the right and left halves. The entire right side of the body is our masculine side (yes, even if you are born as a girl) and the entire left side is the feminine (right, even if you are a boy). Remember, the masculine and feminine have nothing to do with your biological gender. This is a Spiritual concept like 'Shiva & Shakti' of Hinduism and equivalent to the Yin & Yang concept of the Chinese.

However, this distinction reverses in the brain where the left brain is the masculine, and the right brain is the feminine.

Depending on which part of the body takes our focus all the time (or we avert ourselves from it), we can find the secrets of what we are here to work on in this lifetime. And every single secret hides the way back to our discovering our Divine selves.

Having been a healer for over ten years now (and many years in various lifetimes ? Yes, I know), I can positively state that even the quest for 'healing' is a call from the Divine part of ourselves to come closer.

Choosing this lifetime

Every individual is a soul essence of the Universal Soul that has chosen this birth. And as souls we experience life to experience a certain resonance – of Love. It seems the Earth is the realm for only those lives that must or want to experience this one attribute called Love. This is what is also called the 3D level of existence. And yes, there are higher and lower levels of experience. Perhaps on Earth or elsewhere. We will take that up in another journey.

So, when the soul decides to take birth, it realises what it needs to experience, to understand the Bliss of Love. These could be a soul's urge to experience Acceptance, and so choose a life where Acceptance is totally absent and thus create the circumstances for the soul to discover

'Acceptance' in all its flavours. For this, it chooses the parents who will provide it that very experience. These experiences could range from 'abandonment' or 'rejection' to other negative aspects of Acceptance. And we make a soul pact with our fellow soul mates for facilitating the lessons. In the Worldly sense, this could happen as a pact with the higher essences of the soul living (considering the linear version of our life and time) or as an 'agreement' with this soul in the other realm even before this birth. Which again means that these agreements are reached beyond the realm of this time and space.

The pure essence of the soul as it is, comes down and enters the womb of the mother and enters the energy matrix there. This pure essence is no different form the Divine. We are a composite of physical body, emotional body, thought body, Spiritual body etc as we are now. But the soul by itself is pure of all these and is just an aspect of the Divine. These bodies form the sheath which is discarded at the time of death.

We, as one part of the Divine, to experience itself, 'separates' from the Divine, and comes and enters the matrix of energy that is the mother at that point in time. Here we are supposing that the energy of the mother is different from the Divine only for understanding. The 'Divine' for easy understanding here, refers to the pure Consciousness, with none of the additions that happen from the materialistic part. Let us understand that materialism is also Divine later on in this book...

Now let us explore the Sacred anatomy in detail...

CHAPTER TWO

The Mooladhaar Chakra - The Body

Before the energy enters the Mooladhaar chakra, it has to cross the Brahma Granthi, which is a 'veil' of ignorance that is thrown over the Light that enters the physical body.

The Brahma Granthi

The Brahma granthi is a veil of forgetfulness or ignorance that comes into the Divine space of Life that enters the human body. It begins to identify with the body and the surroundings as being separate from the Divine. It makes the body it's territory and makes it the centre of its Observation point – All that is mine.

It is named after one of the God's in the trinity of the Hindus called Brahma.

This veil holds good for the first three chakras and has to break down to allow the soul's journey forward through the next granthi – the Vishnu Granthi that comes up next.

The Mooladhara chakra - Better known facts

The foundation of the body or the being is in the Mooladhaar chakra. Everything that goes into the creation of the person that you think you are, is the energy stored in this Chakra.

The Moolaadhar Chakra is an energy vortex situated at the base of the spine and facing Mother Earth. The Chakra is the densest of all the Chakras. The very foundation.

The Chakra is not a physical phenomenon, so it has not yet been seen by the naked eye. It has however been captured as a 'real presence' within us by advanced techniques like Kirlian photography and much lesser techniques like the Chakra photography equipment that one sees in the local exhibition halls. However, it stands for the solid element of our body or the Earth element.

This is a fully feminine chakra

This chakra is activated by chanting the Bija mantra 'Lam' in C-scale with both our hands placed on our knees with the index fingers touching the thumbs and the other three fingers points outward.

This chakra has been experienced as a four-petal flower facing downwards at the bottom tip of the spinal cord and red in colour.

This Chakra or energy centre leads to the development of the stronger and harder base elements of the body structure like bones, teeth and even hair. It is especially responsible for the health of the lowest part of the body around the anus and covers the hips and legs.

Problems in this chakra can be manifest as issues related to the legs or walking, movement, money, sex for men, ease of flow of blood (blood pressure) and more.

A balanced Moolaadhaar gives a feeling of Abundance (explained below), contentment and Peace.

This chakra is about the sense of smell. This is the first sense organ to develop in the foetus.

This Chakra takes its form as early as the formation of the embryo in the mother's womb. It brings with it all the beliefs of the mother, that this child needs to face in this lifetime. These beliefs are restricted to the beliefs of the mother at the time of her carrying the baby in her womb. This explains the difference in the psyches of different children born to the same mother. And so much more...

Fig 3: The Moolaadhaar Chakra (Root chakra)

Lesser-known facts

The Mother

The mother is the 'Root chakra' is not a wrong saying at all. She is the first being that the baby meets in this Universe when the Divine essence enters the physical body. And this physical body is the mothers.

All the initial effects on this Divine essence are what happens when it is enveloped by the mother's body. The Divine essence which is pristine and pure and totally uncorrupted is Omnipotent and this essence which has come from the Divine is enveloped by the body of the mother which has lived and been corrupted by her life till then. It has the physical elements which are whatever the mother has consumed in her life, her thoughts which have been moulded as per her environment and her emotions which have been modulated as per her experiences till then.

These form the veils for the Divine essence that is the foetus. Every experience that the mother has had and is having at the time of carrying the baby inside her impacts the baby by giving it by giving it the rudiments of thought and emotions and the physical body.

The experience of the mother in the roughly nine months of pregnancy is all the more important as it creates the situation that the Divine essence is here to experience. Every feeling that the mother experiences is teaching the child the way this World is. Every little child has his or her own experience of the World and so sees the World with an individuality that is different from the next. This even explains the differences between siblings and differences and similarities between twins which may be zygotic or non-zygotic - the difference in thoughts and emotions within the mother and where they settle.

Here it is important to understand that even the experiences from the 'masculine' are from the mother and are related to her dealings with her father, her siblings if any and then spouse. It has nothing to do with the father's feelings and experiences or even his Y chromosome. This is one way in which the Wisdom from the chakras is distinct from what science understands till now.

And 'Mother' also becomes our concept of money as we grow up. But more about that later.

Experiences in the womb

What we experience as our root chakra, is formed in the initial stages of our journey when we are in the womb of the mother. This covers the time from conception till roughly six months after childbirth.

The 'separate self' is the pure aspect of the Divine that is in the mother's womb, once it separates from the Divine self. Here it is covered by the physical body, the emotional body, the thought body and all the other bodies of the mother. So, for that period, the 'little' soul shares these bodies with the mother.

During this stage of development, the child is not aware of its distinct self that is separate from the mother. It believes it is the mother and the mother is just an extension of itself. A veil is drawn over the soul's eyes as it is, to keep it unaware of this change from the Divine. The child soul still seeks nourishment from the Source or the Divine. And that is now provided for by the mother.

The soul that inhabits this child, substitutes the Divine with the mother. Whatever it needs to survive – food, shelter, Love, is all provided by the mother. There is no awareness of the passage of time in this stage.

Everything that the mother thinks and feels becomes the thought body and the emotional body of the foetus. Even though it has not learnt the language, the child 'understands' the meaning of the words being spoken or the thoughts the mother is having as a response to the emotions they generate in the mother. The same is felt and acknowledged as 'its own' by the foetus.

These 'feelings' develop into the patterns in the adult. About patterns – soon.

Rooting

Just like the root of plants, the reason for the Moolaadhaar to exist is to 'root' the individual to his human existence. This means, it brings into the space all the patterns that create the oblivion to ones Divinity and bring in the beliefs that entrench the human into the life that he or she chooses. In that sense, it is the first veil.

These thought patterns that make the person forget his Divinity is the knot that was referred to in the previous chapter – the Brahma Granthi. And these are the seeds of the ego. The rest of life is about giving this feeling of separateness or the ego, gratification in various ways, unless and until one embarks on a Spiritual quest.

The growth of the person is affected by the rigidity or the too flowy nature of the roots or these thoughts. So, if people are stuck in the feeling that 'the World is a dangerous place and I clearly need to protect my territory here', that is what the person manifests and if the person subscribes to the view that he or she 'is always taken care of', that is what manifests.

Clearing this chakra helps us in being in the here and now. It is about being present to the connections we have with the World around. Our roots in every space. It is about knowing that however we are, our root always get access to water and nutrients and provides for us. Similarly, we always have access to nourishment wherever we are.

Like the plants and trees in nature, we receive a space to grow from. We may or may not accept the space and hence this leads to flowy nature or rigidity that we have. However, like plants and trees, we too can choose to have roots that are firm and at the same time malleable into the shapes that life throws at us. We can choose to be accommodating and allow the roots to penetrate and reach depths thus strengthening our grounding and not be fixed in the way we think that we become rigid.

Example: We may find ourselves in tough situations, but instead of choosing to run away, we can choose to either take a stand on the problem in front of us and choose to face the consequences.

Let's understand this better...

Patterns

Whatever is the experience of the mother for the period that the child is in the mother's womb, becomes the World view of the child within. For example, if the mother has had a relatively good pregnancy period, supported by her husband and family, the child comes out feeling secure in the World. If the mother has her set of anxieties and worries, the child absorbs the anxieties and worries as the World view.

For instance, a lady who is worried about the way her husband's profession is shaping up will create a child who has worries about the World being ready to support him or her. A lady who is getting physically abused in a relationship will tend to bring a child who has either no hope or is a rebel (reflective of the mother's state of mind). A lady yearning for her husband will cause a child who yearns for male attention. And of course, a happy lady will give birth to a happy infant.

This is not all, even the way the child comes out into this World and his or her initial experiences make up the World view. A child who comes into this World via a caesarean birth and a child via normal birth have distinct experiences which impact it. The child coming from the normal birth is generally self-sufficient and is geared to handle the constraints in life, pushes and finds a way through. While the caesarean births expect an easy life, are not capable of pushing or straining for the things they need. They look forward to being cared for but end up not feeling the same. They are met with the anaesthetised state of the mother and are mostly taken to neo-natal ICUs and separated from the mother in the initial days which leads to the child feeling abandoned. These are of course just examples.

There can also be the case of the premature baby born normally who is also placed in a neo-natal ICU who tends to be a fighter who fights against the World and his or her circumstances and finds a way out in the World on his or her own.

The presence or absence of the father during childbirth also is indicative of the relationship the child will have, to the male parent and thus the elder masculine in its life. The attitude or emotions of the others to the child's arrival also make it feel welcome or unwelcome. A happy welcoming family around will make the child feel welcome wherever he or she goes.

And are these important in the long run? Oh yes. They remain the foundation of the child's belief system throughout life no matter what happens around him or her. These are the beliefs and conditionings which make the child who he or she grows up to be. Which means, it determines the way your average day goes even when you are fifty or looking at the choices before you at seventy.

So, children may be choosing such belief systems that have a problem with trusting people or cannot get along with men or have maladjustment issues with the women in their life throughout based on these patterns that are set in the womb. Of course, children can Choose patterns which benefit them as well.

When we try to make people aware of their patterns, in some cases, it will be so prominent that the person himself or herself cannot ignore it and is convinced of his or her belief, while in others, the person needs to slow down and look at past relationships with people to figure it out.

The child tries to meet its own necessities and tries to make sense from each of his or her actions through the gratification it garners or the lack of it. This gratification is mostly attention from the mother. Depending on how the mother responds, the child begins to define how its attention seeking pattern is going to be. So, if the child gets its nourishment without waiting and is well fed, it is peaceful regarding its Love, food and other needs in life while growing up. If the same is not provided, the child must cry or throw a tantrum to make it happen and that is how the child manages to get support and attention as he or she grows up and behaves even at eighty.

This is one of the reasons that both doctors and the wise advice expecting mothers to take it easy and have a relaxed lifestyle not worrying about anything. It impacts the child that will come out for life.

Breaking patterns

Breaking patterns or beliefs that we have is a three-step process. In the first step, we identify the pattern that needs to be broken. This involves a lot of introspection and investigation trying to understand what happened in our infancy. While some of us may be lucky to have people, who are open to remember and share, we may also be faced with resistance or just the absence of the concerned person in our lives. In such cases, from experience I would ask the person to meditate on the same.

With experience of hundreds of people who have meditated with me, I totally rely on the results of the meditation to see what happened in our lives so long ago.

The method is to set a pure intent to see the answer and then sit in meditation. The process is to calm oneself by observing our breath and slowly bring our thoughts to stillness. Then asking to be taken to the first memory of lack or fear and ask to be taken back to that space and time. See the memory that comes up. The memory itself is not to be judged from the present self or awareness. We need to just accept the memory as it is and come back to the present.

This method can be extended to remember the memories in the womb or during childbirth too as spontaneous memories that come up.

This is because the trauma caused to a child in agony of the mother not having time to look at the child and the agony of a child who has been separated from his mother by death of the mother are not very different. The child just experiences trauma of the unknown. The child tries to explain the circumstance with whatever he or she has experienced till then in life. The fact that the mother is not attending to him or her and not visible can create the same trauma as the child who is experiencing the death of the mother or a dear one. Whatever happened in that moment is of importance and is stored in cellular memory as an imprint of the feeling the child had. It doesn't matter that the mother comes back later in the earlier circumstance. The response to what happened is a trauma which could be caused due to a feeling of rejection, feeling of fear, lack of Trust etc.

The second step is to crystallize the pattern as a pattern of avoidance, rejection, abandonment etc. This also can be tricky as we need to understand the underlying experience well. The trick is to follow through and examine all similar relationships in life that are bothersome. This is because, we do not have traumatic episodes in isolation. It is the very same fear that keeps playing on in our life through various experiences.

Here it is helpful to define and categorise our fear as emanating from what kind of people and what is the trigger of the fear. We can thus categorise our fears from the earliest memory for example, as being of elderly women and triggered by the nature of the words spoken. When we then examine our lives with this, we will see its repetition throughout our life. The 'elderly woman' kept changing but the triggers remained the same and the reaction to all of them was fear. The intensity of fear may vary in these episodes though.

After defining the fear, the final step is the breaking of the pattern by observing our daily routine thoughts and actions. Whenever we realise, we are performing actions coming from a particular belief or fear, STOP.

Look for a counter belief from the Universe. For example, if I believe that my mother always has the habit of questioning where I am going and saying something to hinder the trip, I will need to believe my mother is a happy person (looking for examples when I have seen her happy) and lets me do what I want to (remember a few instances) and appreciates whatever I am doing (remember a few instances).

Here some of you may feel that there are no such instances. But pause! Remember, that is because you are only focussing on one type of behaviour from a person who is capable of having all sorts of emotions! So, it is definitely there. Look for it.

We can set our belief to this new one (in the now) and then look for experiences that substantiate it or just look for experiences that prove our earlier belief is wrong.

The minute we see an instance we should remember to express Gratitude to it. Because, Gratitude is an emotion, that tends to bring back more of the same into our lives. More on Gratitude later. But the sheer expression of Gratitude (whether it is verbally to your mother or even in our mind) makes the belief stronger and the experience, bountiful.

You can support this action by choosing to do opposing actions to your belief. In this example for instance, rather than feel irritated or retort, choose to see her Love and give her Love.

I have just used this one example to explain how to break patterns. The same can be extrapolated to any pattern of thinking.

Try this and share your learnings.

The other energies in the Root chakra

Survival & fears

The phase immediately after childbirth is about the fear of survival. In the aftermath of the veil of ignorance sweeping its folds over the child and thus bringing in concerns or fears about its survival in the World, fear becomes an important emotion that develops in this stage. This could be a mere 'I am not safe here', to 'I am certain of tragedy befalling me'. The 'I' in this case is always the ego and all that it sees as itself. It includes 'my mother', 'my father', 'my job', 'my dog' etc.

People fear illnesses or are ill and continue to live that way again depending on the experience in their Mooladhaar stage of life. Children of mothers who feel over-anxious about the child's health or the child feeling he or she is not supported enough during childhood, invoke illnesses or weakness that make such beliefs true.

Fears of all kinds also manifest at this stage depending on the safety and reliability of the child's environment. These fears could be related to survival, dangers, not getting Love, unwarranted sex, fear of loss of attention and more.

The responses could be flight – escapism or choosing an easy way out. This manifests as avoidance or running away mentally from the World that he or she lives in. Such people either tend to avoid confrontations or are lost in their 'i-Pods' listening to music which numbs their thoughts from thinking about the now.

The second response could be fright or freeze when they become tongue tied or are unable to respond in the situation they face. This fear can be from seeing violence early in life and 'freezing'. These people fear telling their problems and thus feel frozen in the same place. Examples are children mortified from abuse of their self or others.

The third and final response is the fight response which is the rebellion and is experienced as an urge to fight the 'aggressor' and create a space for oneself. This fight may or may not be successful. And such children grow to become rebels or 'fighter cocks' wherever they go fighting for their rights and general living conditions.

The feeling of separation from the Divine also leads to fears. These are the 'lies' that we believe as we do not believe in our own innate connection to the Divine. We believe that we are separate, the Divine is separate and consequently the Devil is also separate from us.

Even though these are lies and can be understood as lies if we dwell on the same, handling fears is one of the most difficult is a layperson's life.

The first step is to identify the fear. This begins with the identification of the physical changes we undergo when experiencing fear. The way the fear feels within the body and the discomfort we feel. At this point it is worthwhile for the person to be in touch with his body trying to focus on where the fear is with his or her eyes closed. Identifying the affected portions and placing one hand on each. (If there are more, choosing the two most affected portions first).

We need to remember that fear is very rarely about the present moment. It is just the physical or physiological response to something that we faced long ago in our lives. These feelings do not leave the body – because we do not allow them to. We avoid the fear and run away from it. Or we freeze under its influence. Or we fight against it. As we can see, all the responses are against it. All we need to do is listen to the body part for the fear to vanish.

Placing a hand on each affected portion when we feel it, we calmly say "I am with you, I hear you" to it and be with the sensations. And as we keep our full awareness on it, the fear "melts away".

The same can be done even when the fear is real and alive outside of you.

Dealing with fears this way helps to clear them out of our system.

Gratitude

As explained earlier, Gratitude is an amazing emotion! It can trigger more of whatever you are Grateful for.

The way to make anything we need, work for us is to simply be Grateful for being provided for with it. This has been hyped enough and more by books like *the Secret*. And it is no different here.

Whoever we are and whatever we may do in life, we truly have a lot to be Grateful for. From our bodies and what parts of them are functional to the simple things that we take for granted like water in the bathroom, food on a plate, a bed to sleep in are all things we can be Grateful for.

There are people out there who live without the things we take for granted! Every single day! Don't you feel Grateful for the things now?

This Universe or Mother Earth, to make it simpler, has provided for each and every one of us. And in fact, she continues to provide what each of us Truly wants. There has been no lack ever and there will be none in the future. The belief is not in a certain amount of money but more in what we need for every moment. For instance, focus on whether you are hungry now and whether you have food. Focus on where you are in your career. Focus on how you are as a person. Focus on how nice you look right now. Find the things you did not see till now.

Just be grateful for what we have every day!

There are people who set about writing Gratitude journals to make it a habit and then realise it. But even holding Gratitude for every single moment in life that we get our due is more than enough.

This also means to remove all habitual patterns of lack, which include hoarding for an unknown future, fear psychosis about 'what will happen if' and investing for a 'bright' future ignoring the present. Look for these thought forms within us and un-condition ourselves.

These simple steps will cause the Gratitude to grow in you.

Abundance

This phase of the baby's development (Moolaadhar) is about his or her connection to Abundance.

The state of Abundance is to feel contentment with being provided for and receiving all that one needs at the time one needs it with no effort and a confidence about this being an expression of life. Truly believing that you will get whatever it is that you need. This is but the original state of this Chakra before the physical body, the emotional body and thought body of the mother covered it.

And the belief of Abundance is found and nurtured in this first phase of life when the mother is feeding her child. If the child is fed whenever he or she needs to be fed, the child becomes 'Abundant'. If the child is overfed, to keep the child from experiencing lack or due to the overconcerned mother, the child grows up to being a fussy about the food he takes and being lazy and laid back, expecting to be fed the things he or she needs. The children who unfortunately experience 'lack' in this stage, due to lack of milk from the mother or circumstantial lack, always yearn for the same. They end up wanting the happy things in life and lacking them always.

So, we have children who will breeze through life with enough money for all times, or people who struggle to make ends meet whether they are in a white-collar job or not. And this feeling continues unless awareness comes in.

So how do we build Abundance within?

By knowing that you are a Divine child like any other whom the Divine will provide for! This needs a lot of un-conditioning the way we learnt to clear patterns.

Also, tidy up the space around you, giving away everything that we do not use for three months or more (taking care of seasonal demands), keeping our transactions clean and giving back all that we owe anyone and keeping only as much as is needed to cover our current needs. Anything more is meant to be given away to those who come and ask for it. Don't worry, they will come.

It is important for all beings to connect to this source of Abundance within. To know that 'I am safe and provided for in this World for every need of mine. I really don't need to think about where it will come from (anxiety) and past experiences (worry). I just need to KNOW that I am provided for always.'

Money

This is the most important aspect of the Moolaadhaar chakra.

Every single emotion we have regarding money, reflects our connection to our mothers. Yes, that is true!

To the new-born baby, the currency for food, needs being met, attention, comfort and Love is the mother. And it is these very same aspects that get transferred to money when we grow up.

Money helps us get food

Money helps to fulfil our needs

Money helps us get attention

Money helps us get comforts

And money also helps us express our Love and feel Loved. (Debatable, but true)

So, it becomes more vital for each of us to have great relationships with our mothers. And if the relationships are affected by other emotions, more reason to heal it. Because you will not experience Abundance, unless you experience Love and completion with your mother.

And yes, when you feel complete with your mother, your Root chakra is automatically healed!

Meditating on the Mooladhaar

Here are various methods of connecting to your root chakra:

1. The Mooladhar or Root chakra as it is visualized as a four-petal flower facing the Mother Earth. It has only one opening – downwards. The colour of the root chakra is red, and it can be aligned by chanting the

beej mantra "Lam" in the C-scale with our entire focus on it. The hand mudra for the root chakra is shown in fig: 4

2. Holding Gratitude and meditating on the Root chakra helps to align it for our highest good and helps us to access its secrets.

3. Another method is to choose a dimly lit area, sit or lie down comfortably with gentle music in the background and gently with eyes closed, run our palm slowly throughout our body starting with the hair on our heads and ending with the toes on our feet. This process can take up to an hour and is worth it. It is also important to linger where the body needs the touch and give attention where it is lacking. The single most important word in this is to be 'slow'.

4. Still another method is to meditate on the Divine Mother (for persons who have a faith) and imagine the Divine Mother picking us up as a baby and feeding us to our Hearts content. Observe the Universe around and the gentle music in the scene. For those interested, the same is available on youtube in our channel – the Truth Vortices.

5. Walking barefoot on the ground for 10 to 15 minutes every day, standing in the tree pose on the ground imagining thick roots sprouting from our feet and going down into Mother Earth and breathing in and out of the feet are methods to enhance grounding.

Fig 4: The hand positions (mudra) for the Moolaadhaar chakra chant

The adrenal glands

Every one of the primary seven chakras has an associated physical entity in the body, which is the physical manifestation post the chakra energy. In the case of the Root chakra, it is the adrenal glands placed above the kidney on either side of the hip.

The adrenals are responsible for the fight, fright, and flight responses in us that we have already discussed. By ensuring that the Root chakra is functioning optimally, the gland secretes its hormone adrenaline optimally which ensures that we have the right amount of energy levels and excitement in our lives at all times.

Any imbalance in adrenaline or nor-adrenaline can be brought back to balance by focussing on the Peaceful state within.

The male sexuality and the Root chakra

The fact that the male sexual organs are in the root chakra and the female are in the Sacral is significant from the perspective of how the race has survived through time. Men have always wanted to increase their chances of being alive past this lifetime by trying to 'sow their oats' in every receptive soil. This means the natural tendency of men is to be polygamous.

Hence, he operates from Fright-Fight & Flight responses rather than loving, caring responses.

However, too much of polygamy and loss of energy as sperms into the World diminishes the potential of the male. For the male to advance Spiritually past the Mooladhaar chakra, he has to be willing to let go of this polygamous nature. He has to respect the vagina in front of him as a Divine space where he chooses to leave his sperm. He has to respect the product created. He has to be responsible for it in the long run. For these facets to be explored and developed, he too has to work on clearing the Sacral of all the energies of domination he has thrust on it over time immemorial.

Then happens the flowering of the Divine masculine.

Health of the Root chakra

The Root chakra is the first stage of development. People stuck in this level of development are faced with survival issues. They either worry about their lack either as money or as health, their own or of their Loved ones.

Their actions are governed by fear. The feelings generally associated with a root chakra imbalance are insecurity, restlessness, lack of energy, suicidal thoughts, etc.

These exhibit in the physical body as aches and pains in the legs, joints, bones, high blood pressure, tremors, issues with the lower spine etc.

The balanced form of the Moolaadhar is one which allows for structure to hold us and guide us but with the flexibility to be changed to a more supportive structure when required. As must be clear, each of the conditioning that we have in the Root chakra is valid and helped us in a particular situation. However, imagine the same being extrapolated to situations it is not required in. That is what has formed as the basis of the root chakra in most humans.

So here's to your creating a new Mooladhar for yourself...

Things you have understood from the chapter

The experiences you have stored in your root chakra (Patterns, your notions of Abundance and fears)

Your way back to the path in the centre (the Sushumna Nadi)

The benefits of healing your root chakra

The right brain way (removing the patterns) & left-brain way (the root chakra meditation and chanting)

The Wisdom of the Root Chakra

- You are born as a spark from the Divine.
- You Choose your mother and your destiny because you Truly want it.
- Every experience has a lesson which needs to be looked for.
- Every thought that you have comes form a belief. If the thought is good, the belief is fine. If the thought is not good, change the belief.
- You deserve nothing less than the very best. If the concept of the Divine is True, it will always care for our need's no matter what. So, it is very important to Surrender them to the Divine rather than bring in our egoistic thoughts.
- Everything is from the mother, which includes every thought, every action, every emotion. And beyond her is the Divine Mother. So, it is important to respect the Divine feminine and hence the feminine in

every form. She will provide, She will take care of us at all times.

CHAPTER THREE

The Swadhishtaan Chakra – The Emotions

Better known facts

The second chakra that develops in us is the Swaddhishtaan. This chakra is about the sense of taste as the name signifies in Sanskrit.

This chakra is a six-petal flower, orange in colour, with two facets. One on the front and the other behind, along the spine and located two fingers below the navel.

This chakra is less dense than the Mooladhar. It is the liquid (water) element in our body.

This is also a feminine chakra

It is activated by chanting the bija mantra 'Vam' in D-scale, with our right hand placed palm facing upwards above the left hand also placed with palm facing upwards on our laps and the thumbs touching in front.

The chakra which is not working to its optimum capacity may result in a person being extremely sexual or totally asexual and with similar problems in the creative space as being either too creative and free flowing or extremely organised and meticulous following the time taught methodologies. Some of them also exhibit as being too addicted either to drugs, alcohol etc or even their work, music, or the like. These tendencies also reveal an inability to adjust to mood swings or handle emotions.

Accepting all emotions and their role in ones' life and being able to express them clearly is the benefit of a balanced Swaadhishtaan.

This phase of development happens when the child is around six months of age till a point of five or six years. Again, these timelines are not hard and fast and can be varied depending on the person.

The Swadhishtaan governs all the adipose in the body and where it is deposited.

This is the stage the child differentiates from its mother's energy body and understands that he or she is a separate individual and needs to take the effort for the mother's attention and Love. Soon, similar feelings separate it from the rest of the world. And these feelings also include the relation the child has, to his or her siblings. These could range from affection to jealousy, control, envy, competition, and victimhood.

Fig 5: The Swaadhishtaan Chakra (Sacral chakra)

Lesser-known Facts

'The other'

After the separation from the mother during childbirth and in the first six months roughly, the child still identifies with the mother on a physical, mental, and emotional level as an extension to his or her own physical, mental and emotional body.

It is only when the mother begins to show affection for things that are significantly different from what the child wants that the baby realises, she is an 'other'.

This 'other' then slowly becomes defined as anybody who thinks differently from the way the baby is thinking. And with this starts the definition of the ego – the borderlines between what is 'me' and what is 'you'. However, this is recognisable as the ego only in the next stage which is in the Solar plexus chakra.

At the Sacral chakra, the 'other' is still someone who 'belongs' to the baby, but who has a mind of his or her own. They have Power over the baby like the baby has Powers over them. And this Power is largely through the attention of the mother or lack of it. This translates into jealousy, envy, control, competition, victimhood.

Experiences in this phase

Pleasure seeking is the main objective of the Sacral child. The minute the child is free to move around, the child explores its surroundings. The child tries to make sense of why his cradle is the way it is, how does it move, how does it feel to crawl, how does it feel to touch the various things around, how do they taste, etc. This is the period when there is curiosity about the entire Universe around. The children in this phase can easily be mesmerised with each new thong that they encounter and are so easily distractable. The feel heat, cold, smoothness, roughness, sweet, bitter, hot, sour, etc. And all these are exciting to it. In later life this pleasure seeking becomes the interest in the opposite sex, interest in Spirituality, etc. The distractions convert to addictions to things that provide excitement. The fascination for the things that provided excitement once, become addictions. But more about that later.

The initial reactions are the awareness of day and night and the passage of time which the earlier child was not aware of. The child begins to recognize the day and the night. The child begins to recognize times for waking up, eating, play and sleeping. And the child also realizes that his or her 'all capable mother' is not his or hers alone. And is perhaps not all capable too.

This is also the stage that the child meets it first 'enemy' - his or her siblings. The child begins to recognize that he or she has a hierarchy in terms of when he or she will receive attention from the parents (yes, the father too begins his journey into the child's awareness). The child also tries and finds ways to get his or her attention past these hierarchies. So, if the child is the eldest, he or she demands attention by doing things to upset his or her parents (that is if his or her parents are not aware), or to play invisible (so that the parent searches for the child) or just by being the youngest one and being used to being catered to for every emotion. Of course, there are many more such options depending on the awareness level of the parents.

This phase is the reason for children to grow up into the leader or rebel, the invisible child or the helpless victim or privileged child etc happens. These are in direct relationship to being the elder, middle, or youngest child or by being treated like one.

Thus, children grow up with stories of how they were privileged or otherwise and the efforts they had to do to survive in the World. These personal stories become myths and larger than what actually is in the mind of the child.

Handling "No"

This is the stage that the child looks at the new world with wonder and delight, giving into its urges of exploration with ease and joy. It uses all its senses to understand the world, predominantly its sense of taste and touch.

Hence the child is busy searching for the various textures and is engrossed in his findings for a long time. Most of the waking hours are spent exploring the world.

As this becomes a stage for the mother to either let her child explore or feel frightened for what happens to the child when he scrambles after a dog or tries to pull out the wire from a socket, this is also the first exposure of the child to the word "no". The feeling to say "no" can also come from the tiredness or boredom of catering to the interests of the little one all the time.

The stage when the child hears the word "no" and learns a coping mechanism for it is important in its life. This is in response to a very positive character of the child to explore. As the child attempts to explore his or her world, there comes many a time when the parent or other elder must step in to prevent a calamity (either real or imagined). At those times, the response shown defines the child in later years. For those children who face a fierce and screeching "no" every time they try something new, the child begins to cringe or quieten and finally either suppresses the urge to explore or does it in hiding.

When the child is awestruck by what he or she sees and is exploring the "World", the parents "no" comes as an unintelligible and fear creating aspect of the World against such explorations. The basic evolutionary urge of "exploring" is cut down to an answer defying "no".

This creates fear for the unknown consequence and a fear to experience pleasure or the thrill of exploration. The impact is lifelong.

And if at this stage the parent attempts to humour the child by lying, the child too learns the art of lying in such situations. The child explains away its urge to explore or explores and tries to hide it behind these lies. The con man or woman births here who cons others into explorative and pleasure-seeking situations.

There is a clearly a misunderstood part of childhood, and the child tries to fathom it and reach a solution which satisfies his or her own image or that of the parent. And thus, begin the stories in the mind of the child for how he or she was manipulated by the 'other'.

For example, the child never does understand why he or she is not allowed to go out of the house all on his or her own self. At this time, the parents may tell him stories about ghosts or people who kidnap children. The child grows up believing these stories and later when his or her belief is questioned, the child is filled with doubt and then begins doubting all that the parents said. Manipulation has become a reality in his or her existence to be used or abused later in life.

Lying and the sacral chakra

When the first trauma of being told "no" happens to the child, the child is extremely traumatised. This is a conflict between its belief of being Abundant and its current state of being told "no, you do not have access to that Abundance". At this stage, the child chooses to "lie" for the first time to soften the blow of what it believed in not being the case.

Children may lie about the thing they were caught playing with either by pretending it is not there, pretending they did not do it, accepting the horrible truth that they did it and face the consequences. These consequences may be trivial and may help them understand the pleasure they were seeking (if their parents are aware or enlightened) or may end being a suffering that is painful.

Accordingly, the 'pretenders' who avoid the damage or thing, become 'avoiders' who run away from things and get involved in something else that deafens out the screams of the lie. They tend to become addicted to these 'somethings' which keeps them away from attending to the reality. These 'somethings' could range from food to music to imagination to creativity to just about anything under the sun that keeps their mind away from the lie.

The 'I did not do it' ones turn into 'liars' who blame the world for the things that "happen" to them. These are the 'victims' who attribute everything that happens to them to a Power outside of them.

And the final lot are the group which does not believe that they are Divine and most often lose their belief in a higher Power as well and hence have to suffer the painful consequence or are the ones who realise there really is nothing to lose and understand their pleasure seeking better.

It is only some of the lucky ones who are told the reason for the "no" and thus retain some of their Divinity.

Emotions

At this stage, the ability to comprehend the World is limited and supported by the basic feelings he or she has when anything happens to him or her. These feelings or emotions are given more weight than they truly carry. They even tend to be exuded by the unconscious mind all through life.

For example, children who are happy on seeing their father come back home (and who are gratified for this behaviour), tend to appreciate, and show their emotions whenever an adult male comes home in adulthood as well. And this later becomes the response to the adult male unless the person has contrary experiences. This is just an example of the behaviour that becomes a part of the unconscious adult responses. There could be many more.

On the converse is the child who is surrounded by over-emotions (from siblings or the parents themselves) and hence sees no value in it and takes refuge in the bitter non-acceptance of emotions.

These emotions range from happiness, pretending to be happy and unhappiness. The unhappiness also can be distinguished as sadness (expressed as tears), sadness unexpressed or just resigned to, sadness that converts to anger, sadness that comes from fear.

The anger can be responded to as irritation, frustration, avoidance, and full-blown anger.

Of course, each of the above can be further classified, but these are the primary types.

In later years, whenever we experience these emotions, they have an anchor in the experiences we had in the Swaddhishtaan or the Sacral periods of our lives.

This is important and pertinent, and we come to realise that all the emotions we eschew as adults are related to or directed to our childhood experiences and not rooted in the current reality. A happy person in an adult situation while mingling with adult males of his or her peer group is just playing out the same experience of childhood with their male sibling. Or attention seeking from the elder feminine is seen in adults who have had not very 'present' mothers.

The emotions of a person are also understood without the utterance of a word. By seeing the expression on any face, one can understand the emotion in the person at most times and by saying that we understand a person more deeply we are conveying our ability to know their true emotions beyond what is seen or expressed.

These emotions also form a body around the physical. This is the reason when you sit close to people for a long time, we tend to take on their emotions too. And this is the reason some homes and spaces have a certain 'feel' to them like desolate, happy, bland etc.

Time

This is the phase when the child begins to understand the concept of time. The baby begins to understand that life is beyond eating and playing (the child is not aware of his or her sleep). The child begins to understand that everything he or she wants does not have to be fulfilled instantly. That it depends on the 'other' person and his or her conveniences as well.

The child understands that the time is divided into the bright days and dark nights. The child gets accustomed to the timing intervals for feeding and changing his clothes.

The child also sees the play of various emotions though not possibly understanding that every emotion is just a temporary state and that every emotion has its place in the cycle of emotions. All the emotions in fact, develop in the Sacral phase.

Sex

The adult experiences with sex are very much related to the childhood experiences in this chakra. The reactions to sex in adulthood are also the same reactions to the explorations and "no" of childhood.

What the child did then will be how he or she handles sex. So, if the child was encouraged to explore, the child confidently explores this aspect of the self. In case where there taboos ("no"s), the child reacts as he or she did to the taboo.

Children who were explained why they should not do something, understood sex, and chose to pursue it within their understanding of the same.

Children who were told a strict "no", either avoided it or tried to do it in a hidden way. And children who discovered the pleasure of what they truly wanted to do by hiding it from their parents, learnt to hide it well and still enjoy it as adults.

The trauma of the unsaid "no" from their end during any sexual molestation also scars them, though this may not be an experience for all children. When the exploration is their body by an 'other'. The tendencies to respond to this also comes from the fears to the consequence. Here the consequences are the thoughts in the mind of the child of not being understood (which comes from being told 'no' many times), of the unknown consequences of these un-understood actions. They do not understand easily that it is ok to say 'no'.

Sexuality and the gender

Another important development in this phase is the understanding that not all people are the same and that they differ based on the sex organs that the body has. This in addition to the pleasure-seeking ability kindled in this phase creates situations for the children to experiment with his or her sexual organs and those of others.

And for the physically female persons, this phase is about understanding the cyclical nature of events starting with their sexual cycles and the recurring nature of periods. The journey of the unfertilised egg from the stage of full maturity to its death once every month and the cycle of the sperm entering the body, the fertilization, the development of the zygote, the foetus and finally the child being born.

Interestingly, the cycle of the egg in the body for each period has a relation with the moon. And this relationship is Sacred. Most people misunderstand this relationship or do not understand it at all. A way to bring back balance in this cycle in the body is by just being aware of the phase of the moon in the sky.

All the person must do (and this is recommended for even men to bring a balance to their emotions as well) is to look at the phase of the moon in the sky every night before going to sleep and closing your eyes and picturing it in your womb area (or Sacral area) shining down on a pool of water. If this is done regularly for a cycle, the cycle immediately begins to synchronise itself to the moon cycle in the sky (Yes, this is true!). And the woman or girl begins to get her periods in synchronisation with either the new moon or the full moon. Even this synchronisation changes once in six months to the other alternative. So, women or girls getting their periods during the new moon tend to get it in the full moon period for the remaining six months.

This process of checking the phase of the moon and imagining it in the Sacral area shining on a pool of water is called the moon meditation.

Whenever the mind is emotional or in any form of discomfort, the tendency will be to see the pool of water as disturbed or with waves or to see the water as muddy. In such cases, it is important to wait till the water settles down and becomes clear. This changes the energy outside too. The very thing causing the irritation or mental disturbance also settles down.

For women with gynaecological conditions, this is even more important as the gynaecological conditions get alleviated over time if this is done regularly.

The sexual glands or gonads

The sexual hormones are the secretions that play a role in the development of this Chakra. The progesterone is of special significance here as it regulates the endometrial lining of the uterus. It also tries to protect one egg and ensure no other egg is competing for the nutrients form the mother.

The function of these along with oestrogen regulates the functioning of this chakra in women.

The cycle of menstruation and how the body moves from being the creator to the destroyer in one complete cycle of the egg brings in the feelings of elation and depression in cycles for the women or extroversion and introversion are the cycles playing out in the feminine body. A well-adjusted person is easy with her emotions and allows them to flow easily in her at any time.

They are also natural care givers being aware of the needs to others and catering to them.

In contrast, men do not have the awareness of the cycles of time naturally. They are not naturally care givers. The body tends to be more muscular in men. However, this difference must be reduced to allow the chakras to work optimally. That is men also need to be fostering and aware of the cycles of nature. This happens when the men also focus on the Sacral and allow it to open up within them.

The end result of the opening of the Sacral chakra for both sexes is a balanced committed coupling with care and protection for the new-born.

Any issues in the sexual hormones can be balanced by brining in the energy of Acceptance and not resisting anything with anyone outside of you.

guilt

This is an important emotion in the Sacral which is not 'real' but troubles and causes maximum hurdles in peoples lives.

The reason it is called 'not real' or 'untrue' is that it is an expression of our Power being in something other than our own selves where it should rightfully be. Once our Power is within us, guilt does not exist. While Power is an expression of the next chakra (Manipura or the Solar Plexus), guilt has more of an emotional cause than a thought as a cause like anger. It is caused by emotions in the other and us feeling responsible for those emotions. This comes about due to felt, perceived or thought-out reactions in the other due to something we have done or not done or thought to have done or not done.

The reality of it is that there is only so much we can do at any given time considering our own presence of mind, our mental makeup, our mental growth our awareness in general. So there really is not need for us to feel we could have done anything any better. If we are placed in the same situation again (without it being a repeated one) things will still happen the same way.

And importantly take back your Power – but more of that in the next chakra.

The inner child

The Truth of the matter is that at whatever stage we live in, we have inner children from the age of the Sacral alive within us. These are the various inner children who have been stopped in their tracks with 'no' or an equivalent action that traumatised the unsuspecting child's thought process as it's 'why' was not answered fully. This is the reason why we feel the way adults react to many situations in a childlike manner unlike their normal selves.

Examples:

An adult who is well educated and trained loses his self confidence in front of his boss and is worried about losing his job in the process. He faces repeatedly insults and derogatory remarks and is tongue tied in the process.

An adult woman who is poised and knows her way around society becomes the loser in a domestic situation with the husband, not quite knowing how to handle him or his bouts of anger. She is a heap of tears and hopelessness.

These situations are just the playing up of the childhood emotions. It is the inner child within them who is active and deserves attention at that moment.

The method to tackle these is also simple. The memories are hidden behind a dominant emotion which was not handled at that time it happened. So, the child has faced trauma and has been frozen in that memory at that time. This child tends to come out when similar experiences happen in adult life. It is he or she who is talking or reacting, not the adult. That is why most people feel disconnected with their emotional selves even after an episode of reactions happen from their end.

When faced with such situations in adulthood, it is best to ask for a few minutes and separate oneself from the incident. Having taken the time, one needs to connect only to the emotion which is generated (ignoring the thoughts that come with it). Now feeling this emotion completely, we ask the body to take us to the earliest memory of what happened. Whatever memory is invoked, we respect it and try to remember what it is.

The memories are generally centred around childhood with something happening to us or a near one. We try and remember why the memory is making us feel the way we do. Then we set right the memory by just offering our self to the inner child (as an adult) and take its permission to make it happy in the situation. The child may or may not be communicative and we need to take care to make it so. If the child tells us what it requires, we do the needful. For example, the child may just want to play with a toy that he or she was prevented from playing with or may want something as bizarre as to shoot dead another family member who is dear to them in the current life.

In such cases, we just do it in the meditation. This process does not require the logic of an adult, but just the escapist fantasy of the child. Thus, we make the inner child Peaceful or happy. The child's 'trauma' is taken care. The child is now ready to assimilate back into you.

At the end of the meditation, we feel the Peace that the child feels and breathe it into all parts of our body. If the child is ready, we allow it to become one with us again. By merging with us, the energy of the child is present with us as an adult, to be harnessed when required.

And this is not a one-time process. We need to do it every time we face an unhealed emotion in the present time. And as we heal the inner children, we find a happier and content adult emerge within us.

Values, desires and passions

This being the stage that the child experiences emotions for the first time and experiences desire for certain things (which are being kept away from him or her), the child gets a motivation to act. The very act of an adult giving a certain thing of value makes it desirable.

This makes the person approach the thing of desirability with a passion or passion-less-ness. This results from the object being kept desirable, made undesirable without explanation (which invokes desirability in the child) and made wholly undesirable (where the child begins to have a negative feeling for the same).

The first and second options create a passion in the child to experience the object and this drives the child to action. These may be overt or covert action depending on the passion generated being positive or negative.

The same becomes the way the person looks for similar objects in his lifetime. Children develop differently depending on whether they have been similarly encouraged to go after material things or not. So, children who have been taught that running after material things is 'not okay', grow up and tend to ignore money and material possessions. While children who have been encouraged for the same, accept these easily and enjoy them too.

Similarly, the child who has been told that it is exciting to indulge with the opposite sex, but that it requires the other sex to appreciate us, develops a passion for them without feeling embarrassed about it. And such an adult also waits or looks for the reciprocity before proceeding and does not indulge in force.

Relationships

All the relationships that we dream of, want, run away from are all centred in this Chakra. The attraction that a child or a teenager or a person feels for another is just the imbalance in the chakras calling out.

While most people are fixated by 'that one person', these rules apply for all relationships. I will use 'that one relationship' here to explain.

We relate primarily only to our parents. Our mother is an archetype of the expectations we have for all of womankind and our father signifies our relationship with the masculine.

Whether we like it or not, that is exactly what we manifest.

Depending on the energy that we have given to these relationships, the sexual attraction is to the parent's sex who has been 'lesser loving' in the childhood. This can also be a perceived lesser loving presence. So, children with a quiet and workaholic mother invite reclusive women into their lives whom they are not sure of in terms of their emotional status.

Children with aggressive fathers or not present fathers manifest an excessive anxiety to please the masculine and this tends to affect their later lives in not dealing with this aspect of the father.

Even the person we choose as a sexual partner is either a carbon copy of our other sex or same sex parent or an exact opposite. That is to say, if we were bothered by an aggressive father figure in childhood, we choose a partner who is an exact opposite. Or in some case, we invite the same energy back into our lives. This is even true of arranged marriages and love marriages.

The action is something as follows. Our energy centres send out a vibration which attracts the equal and opposite charge to us. This might initially be experienced as 'love' or infatuation for the more aware, where we see the perfect partner in them and present the perfect partner in us to them. The issues to be faced surface only after the relationship is moving ahead.

Even the attraction we find for a certain kind of man or woman is a response to the energy from our energy centres. It is these very centres which attract and repel beings based on our experiences.

Water retention and the Sacral

Sacral is about the water or liquids in us. This can be as the flowing emotions or as plain water. Water as you know forms 80% of our physical body. The changes that we undergo every hour of the day is a response of this water being 'pulled and pushed' as the case may be and the various emotions flowing through our body.

When the moon is able to pull and push the oceans into tides every single day, can we mere mortals be much different?

If we tend to not drink enough water, we tend to become 'drier' in terms of emotions and if we drink too much water, we tend to allow our emotions to flow uncontrollably. The water may also tend to linger in our bodies as swelling or oedema. This results from conditions where we are not allowing our emotions to flow freely and are clinging on to it.

Emotions are just meant to flow. They do not belong to us or to anyone. They are just meant to flow through. Suppressing or controlling any kind of emotion whether it is happiness or anger, or resentment is a sure-fire way to invite deadly diseases like cancer. And the way to control or survive cancer is also to let go of the control of the emotion concerned.

While I have mentioned this rather lightly here, it is very much possible to cure cancers by going to the depth of the emotion that is suppressed and setting it free by understanding which part of the body it is in and what the suppressed part is telling us by its position, pain etc.

Meditation on the Sacral chakra

Focussing on the six-petal flower on either side of the spine (front and back) which is orange in colour and chanting the beej mantra "Vam" to the D-scale helps to activate or energize this chakra.

As this chakra is about the soft tissue in our body, it also helps to dance sensually with the movements of the hips emphasized. Imagine being in Love with the Universe and the Universe returning the Love to us. Move as if you are dancing this secret sensual dance with your Divine partner and the partner is making us feel really sexy.

Creative channelling is also a great meditation. We could plan sketching, or painting or singing or dancing with an abstract beginning which could be just a shape on the piece of canvas. The rest of the meditation could involve creating something from the shape. If we choose dance, we could begin with dancing to unfamiliar but beautiful music, allowing our body to find the way with each step. If music, we could just start with a raag or a tune and sing from there till we reach wherever possible creating as we go.

Swimming in water or just meditating in water is another means.

It is important to keep our mind focussed on what we are doing in all these cases.

Fig 6: The hand position (mudra) for the Swaadhishtaan Chakra

Meditation on the inner child

Sit down in a comfortable space with your spine erect and focus on your breath. Observe the air as it moves in and out of your body. Take your attention to those parts of the body that are still calling to you and trying to divert your attention. Say 'I am with you', mean it and continue saying that till the distracting pains of other feelings melt away.

Focus on your spine as you breathe in and out and allow your Consciousness to enter the Sacral point along your spine.

Enter a large orange room which seems to be circular and walk towards the centre of the room. You will find a child there in the centre. Walk up to the child.

Is the child a boy or a girl?

Does the child look happy or sad?

Is the child paying attention to you?

Go up to the child and sit down next to it. Pick it up if it is still a baby. If not, just be with it.

Ask it if there is anyway you can help the child (At this stage if the child says 'no' or doesn't say anything, stay put for a few minutes more, thank it and come out of the meditation. You can repeat the same the next day as well and ask it the same question. It eventually will ask you for your help)

If the child answers with what it wants, just listen attentively and unconditionally.

Whatever it is that the child needs, do it for the child. (As mentioned earlier, these requests may be as frivolous as a wanting a particular flower or chocolate to killing you). Remember, it is important to let go of our Worldly connections and feelings and just do it for the child.

Once the child is convinced that what you have done is complete and that it has received its due, it will be happy. At this time ask it if you can hug it. If yes, hug the child and feel the Love for the child. If the child is really happy, ask it if it is ready to assimilate in you. If yes, breathe in long and deep. Feel the energy of the child entering you and assimilating in every cell of yours. Continue to breathe deeply till you feel the assimilation is complete.

Sometimes the child may not be ready for the hug or may not be ready to assimilate. That is perfectly ok. Thank the child and come of the meditation. Do the process again the next day till the child completely assimilates in you.

When you feel the process is complete in a meditation for the day, rub your palms and place them over your eyes. Gently open your eyes.

Remember, we have infinite inner children within us who have got stuck in perceived traumatic moments. Our own energy is stuck in those moments as these inner children. So, it is important to liberate as many inner children as you can.

Meditation on the Moon

This meditation is to be done just before going to sleep.

Sit down cross legged with an erect spine in a comfortable area with your eyes closed. Observe your breath and bring your mind to stillness. If thoughts come up, bring the attention of the mind back to the present moment and Observe your breath.

When the mind is calmer, enter your Sacral through the spine. Visualize a vast body of water there. See the moon as it is in the night sky shining on this body of water. See this scene till the body of water becomes still. (This may take some time initially and on some days in between. Tha tis perfectly ok. It just reflects your out state of mind)

Once the water is still and you can see the Reflection of the moon on the body of water, feel Gratitude and slowly exit the meditation.

Health of the Sacral Chakra

A healed Sacral chakra or Swadhishtaan means a person comfortable with his or her sexuality, who is freely creative and responsive to the World at large. The person is also committed to his partner and lives a balanced life with emotions, accepting all of himself or herself.

The unhealed aspects exhibit as putting on fat or losing fat, issues related to the adipose tissue, issues related to our sexual anatomy and genital hormones (ovarian cysts, reproductive issues, impotence), lower back pain and pelvic issues.

Things you have understood from the chapter

The experiences you have stored in your Sacral chakra (Pleasure seeking, lies, trauma, jealousy)

Your way back to the path in the centre (the Sushumna Nadi)

The benefits of healing your Sacral chakra

The right brain way (healing the inner child) & left-brain way (the Sacral chakra meditations and chanting)

The Wisdom of the Sacral

- Emotions are the expression of desire in various forms. They flow and should not be stopped. Hence, Accept all emotions
- Stoppage or control of emotions results in diseases
- Pleasure seeking is a Divine nature. Accept it in all its innocence and wonder
- Due to the development of the ego, we continue to fight out battles of our inner child which has been traumatised in life so many times. Heal the inner child and free it – experience the new energy.
- Acceptance of every other in your life is an Acceptance of the Divine energies within you

CHAPTER FOUR

The Manipura – The Thought body

The better-known facts

The Solar Plexus Chakra is also known as the Manipura Chakra or "The city of the Jewel" as is the literal translation of the word Manipura. This chakra is yellow in colour and the element here is fire.

This chakra is situated two fingers above the navel along the spine and has two openings on the front and the back. The chakra itself has been visualized as a yellow fragrant flower with ten petals in it. It is activated by chanting its bija mantra "Ram" in E-scale with our hands placed in 'namaste' position with our fingers pointing away from the body.

It represents the element of fire within us.

This is the first purely masculine Chakra.

It governs the muscular tissues in the body and is about control. This is also the chakra where the ego matures and takes charge in our life.

This chakra is related to sight. It helps us 'see' the World as per the way we are ready to see it (patterns).

Ego has always been classified as a negative word with negative connotations. For this book, we will accept ego as it is - Unconditionally. It is just the protective aspect of ourselves to save our beliefs systems which have protected us in the past.

This chakra is associated with all the problems that we faced when the ego is pitted against the other in the World. So, it causes digestive issues like indigestion, acidity, ulcers, gall bladder stones, tumours in the colon etc.

A balanced Manipura exhibits calmness, centred people who are in balance with the World and are very successful.

Fig 7: The Manipura Chakra (Solar Plexus chakra)

Lesser-known facts

The ego

The Solar plexus stage ranges from approximately three years to six years of age. This stage is about the development of the ego.

This includes the development of the child when the child steps into school or mingles with the big outer world. When the child enters school and meets other children from families the child has not met, it for the first-time occurs to the child that he or she is not the centre of the Universe and that what she or he is encountering is not "mine" in any sense of the term.

These children seem similar but have their own set of parents, their own vehicles, their own belongings and seem to interact independent of others. Importantly, these children have the Power to cry and be heard which is not related to the ability of our child for the same. And the person's caring for or protecting these children are both known and unknown people. Our child is at best an equal to it.

At that time, each child tries to classify the world into perceivable bits like "My bag", "his book", "her pencil" etc. This goes into the myriad of experiences that the child has. And each of it is classified as "better than", "worse than", "equal to", "same to same" etc. These are the first elements of comparison rising within the child.

Each child develops its own coping mechanism in this scenario. The children range from extremely sweet or notorious in their approach to handle these situations.

Fortunately, or unfortunately, most of our behaviour learned in this stage, exists to this date when we are much older. And the point is that we are unaware of them. We are unaware of the fact that we have this comparison matrix running within us and are classifying and judging each thing that comes into our space as being "good" or "bad" based on these previous experiences. This becomes the reason for our prejudices and our expectations, none of which are in front of us. At the best, they are somewhere on the side angles of our vision. We are not aware that everything we see and classify is being compared as per this old method.

The journey through this chakra is about becoming aware of this concoction called the ego and learning to break it down till we become just our wide-eyed, wonder filled selves, even beyond the emotions that have come to stay.

Imbalances in this chakra result is people being maladjusted to their surroundings, always at loggerheads with the others around. Health wise, it results in acidity, ulcers, liver or bile issues, diabetes etc. This can happen from both under action and over action of the chakra. We can have over aggressive people and victim mode people due to its imbalance.

Experiences in this phase

As a part of the learning that happens in this chakra period, the child is creating a map of experiences and thus his or her position in this matrix and thus defining his or her ego.

The child's focus is his or her own self and the focus on the external is just to fix a position for himself or herself in relation to the "other".

The inclination or curiosity to know the new with wonder is watered down with doubt and conditioning. The child is "bored" or "wary" of the new frontiers. The focus becomes to define one's own boundaries with the new. Am I the king or Queen or the follower? How does the new finding impact me and my boundaries?

When the experience is positive, it is accepted exagerated and when it is negative, it is ignored, run away from or outright denied.

The naming of the ego elements and the descriptors of one's world are enhanced and added to every conversation in the mind or outside.

For example, the type of teacher that a student has is classified based on experience as 'good' or 'bad' based on how they are to look at (connecting to previous experiences with such people), gender (bias), accent (good, educated or otherwise) and the added new experience of the session as it is. The impression generated sticks to the person and forms a basis for future experiences despite the subsequent experiences with the same teacher. Hence, we all have the loveable teacher, the strict one, the knowledgeable one etc which are based on one or two instances of the said behaviour which came up initially in the interaction.

The reason for our doing things also is coloured by the ego. The children who are motivated to study and behave well, do so and appreciate the same, while those who are not given gratification for their marks or proficiency in studies, ignore the same in their own self and others.

Similarly, those who are exposed to women who work and are accustomed to seeing women take decisions at home tend to respect women and their decisions when they grow up as against those who see only a submissive figure or a person whose decisions are overridden by the significant others at home. And in their egoic hierarchy, they are placed equal to, below or above women. (The origin of patriarchy, both within girls and boys).

The ego thus creates a space around each individual that is distinct from other individuals. This space which is about all the 'do's' and 'don'ts' that are acceptable to the person and this space is generally not crossed over by any other individual or actions which contravenes it. Even when a loved one crosses any of these definitions, the ego rebels to it and the loved one is pushed out of the 'intimate' zone.

Interestingly, all these are just the protective devices of the ego to take care of the person when his or her boundaries are threatened. Thus, ego is just a protective device. And none of the facets of the ego is created with a reason beyond this. However, the insignificance of the boundaries laid out is lost as time goes on and people stick to the boundaries till it is questioned and conquered – with Love.

The person tends to behave from within the ego in most circumstances and limits his or her own consciousness within it. The way out of ego fuelled situations is for the person to step out of the ego and examine his or her boundaries. And when the consciousness is expanding, the boundaries do too.

Thoughts

The important development in this phase of the child is the emergence and onslaught of thoughts (the very cause of ego). Thoughts – which are formed from language are distinct from emotions. These condense the story of what happened to the person through ideas and verbal picturizations and combines numerous emotions without having the need to express any one of them (though some of them may be expressed as well). Thus, they have the complexity of combining emotions with thoughts.

Hence, the thinker associates certain thoughts with certain emotions and thus understands things. But the thought of the thing is corrupted with the associated emotion. So, we have happy flowers, sad flowers, detesting flowers, angry flowers etc, based on the correlations that the person has with them.

And thoughts have an existence of their own spawning new thoughts and keeping themselves alive. This can lead to a thought about needing to buy a pencil leading to feelings of low self-esteem from the result of a person's last exam and thus hating the people who scored above him or her and of course, carry on from there.

Thoughts are fundamentally only meant to serve the purpose of language and communication. But due to this nature of self-creation, they sustain and create a body around the person which in most cases controls the way a person thinks or acts.

Anxieties

These are again thoughts as we discussed, created from fears. Fear of things going wrong. Fear that what has been done is not enough. Fear that we have lost control of the situation. And that the result of these fears has not yet manifested. We 'fear' the worst and hence project this belief into the world.

The thing to remember here is that it is all imagined. Every single anxiety we are having of a situation is a negative expression to the Universe. It basically means we do not Trust any higher Power. We do not Trust that we will be taken care of and that everything will go fine. The little ego within us is expecting things to go a certain way.

And most importantly, we are in the future when we are anxious. We are not in the present. The present moment is still untouched, pristine. There is nothing to cause anxiety in this moment. And it is ok to be here.

There is no situation in the World which is completely in our hands. If nothing we need the help of the people to create the things or change things around us. It could be a chair or an air-conditioner, we still need someone to help us 'make things happen'. And remember, this is not taking into consideration the Divine. And there are at any given point so many ways things can be done. We just need to know that the Divine is in charge and is working along with us. The 'doing' is limited to what we need to do and then Trust the higher self or higher energies and relax. The added 'thinking' as anxiety is not helping anyone, not even you. And importantly the Divine is noticing our lack of Trust in it – and so not acting and allowing our ego to takeover.

The answer to anxiety is of course to let go, relax and enjoy the journey Trusting the one above (or below or wherever!)

Worries

Similar are the nature of worries. These are about things that have passed. Hence, we worry about how they have impacted things in the past and the repercussions we have faced, are facing or will face.

These again are imaginary repercussions of the past deed or happenings and are not rooted in reality. The focus on the negative is only creating an energy matrix for the same to be manifested. These do not help us in anyway. Again, there is a lack of Trust in the Divine being the 'doer'.

No past event has the propensity to become the "way the world is". We make it that way by worrying about them. By letting go, we just allow each incident to remain just that – an incident, with no Power to manifest further.

Our basic nature is to be concerned about things. And by concern, we confuse it to mean 'worry about it'. Even if you take the things we Love into consideration, by not Trusting the Divine and not Trusting that all things will be taken care of, we try to bring in our ego to take control of the situation and 'do' the 'caring'.

The greatest things created, the happiest persons, the awesome holidays seen and experienced are rarely due to planned caring, it is just by Loving the journey and the end result.

Anger

This is the hallmark emotion of the Solar plexus. And it includes a whole range of feelings from irritation to anger to scorching fury. Incidentally anger is the burning (setting on fire) of the boundaries of the ego when it is threatened.

It is the distress caused within the body when one of the protective measures of the ego is challenged. The person does not stop and think and so fights the onslaught of the new idea or thought that is challenging the status quo.

And as this is a heating energy from the digestive juices it creates havoc in the stomach and intestine areas over time. It burns down the wall of the stomach and intestines and causes ulcers which over time may lead to further problems like stomach cancer.

The way to deal with anger is to pause, stop thinking and to just breathe slow and deep. Touch all the parts of the body where you feel the anger and just say "I am with you" to each part (and mean it). Once the feelings subside, come back to the situation, and look at it. You will have your answer and the 'boundaries' of the ego will be broken. Take my word for it. Try it... ?

shame

This is again a state of Powerlessness due to a situation being caused where we feel utterly Powerless in comparison to some others, and we are exposed in our vulnerable state. There seems to be no way that the others do not perceive our Powerlessness. The vulnerability and the perceived situation in these cases are real in our head.

These are spaces which were never filled with substance that stand exposed for what they truly are. However, these situations are always created by the ego. For instance, for a person who has Accepted her or his own self completely and is fully in his or her Power, shame cannot be caused as it is a Powerless state. So, this person will not experience shame due to any part of her or his persona being exposed. He or she will already know it and will have Accepted it.

The full-fledged ego

The ego is one of the features of the Solar Plexus or Manipura chakra. The ego as explained earlier, is the protective part of us when we realise that we are separate from our mother. It is the part of us which creates boundaries between what we feel is our territory or area of dominion and that of the 'other'.

However, we tend to leave those boundaries intact and never expand them or obliterate them. And that causes the issues we face in daily life when anyone steps into the ego zone. We then have to define them as a friend or foe and choose to entertain them or declare war (of course both are extremes, but the space created is between the two).

The ego controls.

And in this control drama between individuals are formed the two types of individuals – the victims and the aggressors.

Victims are those who allow their Power to be taken away and are often found with their Power in other things. For example, they allow the thoughts about others to dominate their psyche. Whether the other person is happy or sad, whether what they are wearing will be liked by everyone else, whether what they are studying will make their parents proud etc. And they tend to compensate for the same. They change their worlds for the benefit of the 'others'.

Aggressors are the persons controlling the victims (at least in the victim's minds). However, they are not very different. Their thoughts are all about how to make the victims around do their bidding. And in seeing this they feel the Power (which is Truly not theirs). The Power here is also in the other – the victim. What irks them is the refusal of the victims to comply. Though victims generally do not know this, even a small attempt at rebellion by the victim is enough to make the aggressor disturbed. So, in that way, they are victims too. However, they are control freaks and do not like to have their worlds changed from the way they think it ought to be.

Interestingly, the aggressor also walks around as the protector. They are the very same. They cannot survive without a victim to protect or a victim to aggress on. The same applies here. The protector becomes agitated and takes on the role of the aggressor should the victim Choose to rebel or even be Free.

The aggressor – victim modes can even be softened slightly to make them the aloof (aggressor who pretends not to want the attention of the victim) and the snoopy person (who is forever interested in the goings on in the life of the aloof person). The rest of the story is the same.

It is all about the Powerplay of the control freaks and the easily controlled. And all of these are just thoughts.

The Pancreas and the digestive hormones

The digestive hormones and the pancreatic juices digest whatever enter the body through the mouth. Energetically they act on all the information that enters the body through the brain and 'digest' it. So, even as food is digested and waste materials removed, the information is processed, waste is removed, and the rest of the knowledge is retained.

So, when the ego resists any thought, word or action in the outer world, it upsets the functioning of this chakra. This resistance leads to more acid being secreted into the gut and the lining of the stomach and intestines being corroded.

Any issues in the production of insulin (secreted by the Pancreas) or any of the other digestive hormones can be corrected by Observing the ego and where it is stuck.

Who am I?

Are we the ego? Are we the name that we carry? Are we the things that we do? Are we the family that we belong to? Are we the degrees that we have earned in life?

In Truth we are not any of these. These are just the definitions we came up as we grew up to define what we are. We are none of these.

We are not happy all the time. We are not angry all the time. Neither are we any other emotion all the time. Yet we describe ourselves as happy-go-lucky, brilliant, creative person or some other such definition which can even be a Powerless, unconfident person. Are we these at all times? Have we not experienced the contrary? We are none of these either.

In Truth we are nothing. NOTHING at all. Everything we have or had has an expiry time including the present life. Nothing is permanent. Everything changes. As do we.

However, if we meditate on this nothingness and focus on it, we can reach the Power of anything. Yes, we also have the potential to be anything in this World. You just need to Choose what you want to be and go for it. So go person, GO!

Power & Choice

The True meaning of Power is that which is alive in all of us as the will to live. It has nothing however to do with the Power in another. There is a World where the Power in one Person does not threaten that in another – and that is the real World.

Power is that state where one knows that one has a Choice at all times. The awareness that each step in life is a Choice that we make out of a myriad of Choices.

So, when you make Choices in your life taking full responsibility for the consequences, you are in your Power.

When you Truly understand this, you Choose the life of your dreams. Yes, sometimes it may be about being a victim, but be a victim by Choice, knowing that you have the Choice to change your mind.

Taking back one's Power – A meditation

Sit down in a quiet place with your spine erect and Observe your breath. Just watch it unconditionally as it moves in and out of your body. If there are parts of your body calling out for your attention, attend to them. Be with each part and tell it "I am with you" repeatedly (and mean it) till the pain or disturbance calms down.

Take your attention to your Solar plexus on your spine. Enter it with your imagination. You enter a large vast space that looks like a circular room and is rather well lit in the centre. Walk towards that well lit centre and sit down the way you are seated now (cross legged and with erect spine).

Become aware that there are many people, places, times and things with which you have left your Power in the past who are now present outside you in your own Solar Plexus. Let the Power you left behind in these people, places, times and things connect to your Solar Plexus as thin chords. Feel them pulling at you from various sides.

Each of them is a space where you left your Power. The energy of the person you have become is much lesser than what you were prior to these incidents. So, it is important to claim your Power back in all these cases.

Meditate on the light shining above your head and express your intent to the Light (or Divine) that you are ready in this space and time to cut the chords with these Power draining experiences. As you meditate, imagine a Powerful sword of diamond come down from the Light and gently drop into your hands.

Pick the sword up and cut the chords one after the other close to their origin in your Solar Plexus. As you keep cutting these chords, feel the Freedom and the loosening of the strings. Cut away until there are no strings attaching you to those experiences.

Now fold your hands in prayer and thank the people, places, time and things for the experiences you had with them. Express that you do not need them in your Power space anymore. Ask them to leave. Remember, even if you see people whom you Love at this time, request them to leave as this is your Power space.

You will see all of them leave Peacefully and with their own Power replenished.

When the last person leaves take a few deep breaths and feel your own replenished energy. Continue to breathe and allow this energy to circulate into each and every part of your body.

Once you feel complete, gently rub your palms together and place the warm palms on your eyes. Slowly open your eyes.

Observation or Witnessing thoughts

This is the most Powerful method which indirectly controls thoughts and thus the mind and thus the Solar Plexus chakra. However, any attempt to control your thoughts only makes them more aggressive.

All we need to do is to observe the thoughts (witness). As we witness thoughts, we do not judge them. We can of course label them for convenience. For this, we just watch each thought as it plays out in our mind. And label them - "Hey, there is a thought on the weather", "there is a thought on pain", "there is a thought on unfinished business", "there is a thought on low self-esteem", "there is a thought on my observing the thought".

As we do this exercise, we come to realise the witness stance. This witness within us, which is observing the thoughts, is distinct from the thought. It is not the thought. It can see the thought as a separate entity. And as it is just a witness and non-judgemental, it does not involve with the thought or engage with it.

And as we Observe or Witness thoughts, they slowly slow down and eventually disappear.

This is very Powerful even when we are experiencing an emotional breakdown. If we can bring ourselves to the Witness stage, we can Observe the thoughts and as we Observe them, calm them down. Even during the worst crisis that we may be experiencing, the actual problem that we are facing are only these - thoughts. And Observing them, brings down their effect immediately.

The thoughts are either anxiety about the future (yet to happen) or worries about the past (already happened and so cannot be changed). When we recognise this, the thought loses its ability to alter our emotions. And in due course calm down.

Meditation on the Manipura Chakra

The main meditation for this Chakra is the 'Witness' stage or the 'Observation' of thoughts. We sit comfortably, cross legged with an erect back and hands clasped in our lap. We observe the normal breathing that is happening in our body. We watch the breath as it enters the body, moves down and fills the space, the pause and the flow back of the return of the air to the outside followed by the final pause.

As we observe these, thoughts will tend to come in. We just observe the thought when we notice them, label them, let go and return to focussing on our breath.

We continue this for as many minutes as the years of our age. Example, a five-year-old does it for 5 minutes while a 27 year old does it for 27 minutes.

This meditation is also called the Aana-paana sati.

Make Aana-paana sati a habit. Experience your Power enhancing with each session of Aana-paana-sati.

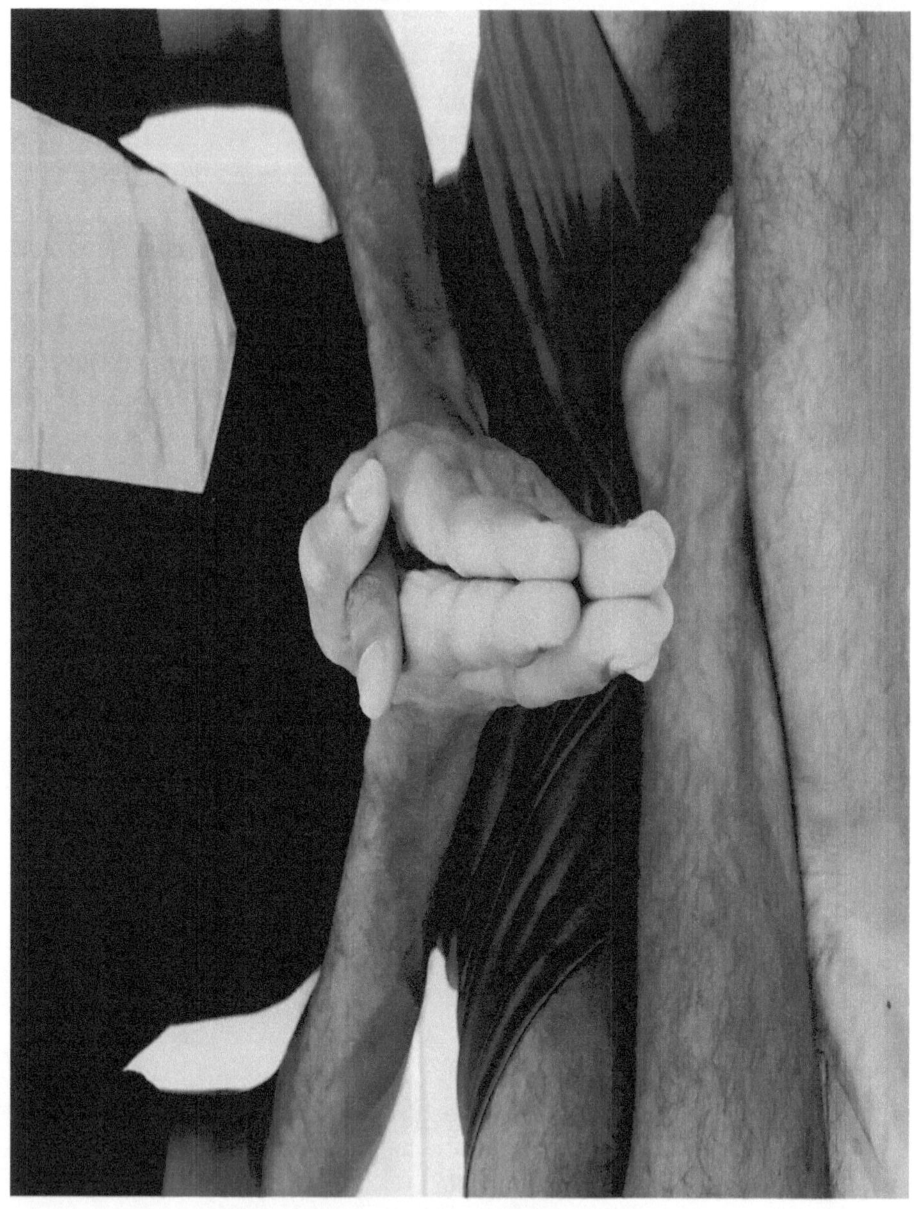

Fig 8: The hand positions (mudra) for the Manipura Chakra

The Sun meditation

Just as we had the moon meditation in the Sacral, we have the Sun meditation in the Solar Plexus. The essence is to bring in the Power of the Sun into our actions and do them like the Sun – Unconditionally and without attaching any thoughts.

Close your eyes and sit down in a cross-legged position with an erect spine. Observe your breath (as done in the earlier meditations) till you feel settled.

Once you are settled, imagine the Sun shining brightly in the middle of your Solar Plexus. Feel the rays shining out of you. Breathe the Sun into your Solar Plexus in such a way that it becomes a permanent energy in your Solar Plexus. Feel the radiance shine out of your being into the World outside. Hold this feeling till you feel complete.

Rub your palms and place them over your eyes and then open your eyes.

The 'who am I' meditation

Meditate on what you think you are. Question it. If you find something again, question that too. Keep going till you experience what is being nothing.

This meditation may take time or may happen in one sitting. However, for your own Spiritual growth, it is important to do it.

The Wisdom of the Solar Plexus

- We are not the ego
- We are not anything we think or do
- We are nothing
- In that nothingness is the potential to be anything

CHAPTER FIVE

The Anahata chakra – The Love centre

The Heart chakra or the Anahata chakra, is the one without a sound or before a sound disturbs it. It also means stillness. Hence it is referred to as the unstruck" or "unbeaten" or "unhurt" part of us.

Entering in the Anahata mode of living is a blessing. A transition from the ego centric existence we had till we were in the Manipura. It is that stage of life when the child in his teens or during his puberty and afterwards.

The Vishnugranthi

In between the Manipura and the Anahata chakra there is a granthi called the Vishnu granthi or the knot of Vishnu. This is the veil of the ego and the separation of 'I' from others.

The people who are more lower chakra centric find it hard to imbibe this Wisdom that we are all interconnected. People who cross over to the Heart Chakra or the Anahata level of consciousness realise that they cannot exist without the others. And that for existence to be smooth and transformational we will need to let go of the ego and its controlling ways.

Makes sense, doesn't it? It makes the saying "If you Love something, set it free, if it returns to you, it is yours, if it does not, it never was!" (We will examine the later part of this statement, later on in this chapter itself).

The better knows facts

The Heart chakra or Anahata is green in color and is the air element within us. It is visualized as a flower with twelve petals and has a face pointing into the body from the spinal cord and another facing away from the body to the backside of the person in the region of the Heart.

This Chakra has both the masculine and feminine parts equally and there is a merging of these energies in the fully developed Chakra.

The mantra to activate this Chakra is the beej mantra "Yam". This is to be chanted with the right hand on the heart in the mudra with the index finger folded and thumb joined and the middle and ring fingers and the little finger is free and pointing outwards and the left hand in the chin mudra at the left knee. We are to be seated with crossed leg and an erect spine.

Activating this chakra awakens the awareness that we are dependent on the 'others' to be complete. Or that the 'I' does not end with us.

Let's examine the physiology to understand this better. Just like the organs of this area (the Heart chakra), the lungs, do only half the work of oxygenation in our body, the oxygen for the same is derived from the plants out there. So the cycle is complete only when this oxygen reaches us and is processed through the lungs, through the alveoli, through the blood stream into the Heart and taken to each cell within where it is used up for the cellular activities and the carbon dioxide that is generated is released into the blood streams, carried back to the heart where it is pumped back into the lungs and the alveoli where it is exchanged for oxygen once again and the released carbon dioxide reaches nearby plants and is absorbed by them to be converted to oxygen and water through the process that we call photosynthesis. That actually, is the complete breathing mechanism of each of us. We are fully dependant on each green plant for our existence!

This chakra helps us helps us feel with the sense of touch.

Even the Heart and the circulatory system are about pumping the pure blood to different parts of the body and collecting the impure blood from them. So, they too are not about that specific location.

When the Heart chakra is working optimally, the person experiences Love is all its Purity for every living and non-living thing around.

Problems in this chakra can give rise to blood cell conditions like anaemia, poly-cytaemia or lung related issues like Asthma, COPD, tuberculosis, lung cancer etc.

Fig 9: The Anahata Chakra (Heart chakra)

Lesser-known facts

The experiences during this phase

This phase begins around puberty and continues to the end of teenage. This is the phase when the child first 'sees' the 'other' with craving and passion. This is the time when crushes occur. When the fascination for an 'other' makes the young person forget himself or herself.

The ego is crushed. And the person celebrates the other and sees the other as being a very special person. Everything that was her or his own are now considered 'ownable' by the other. And everything owned by the other become deified. There is a freeing of the energies that were under the control of the ego.

The person wants to move out into a group of friends of her or his own age, the person tries new food, new clothes, new things that are 'cooler' to try out like substances not considered kiddy and may include substances like cigarettes, pot, drinks etc (and all the numerous things that are addictive), new ways to deal with the World and all the other strange things that come with 'growing up but not grown up enough'. All these tendencies are just the energies trying to free themselves.

Now if the 'other' does not reciprocate the same feelings, it is followed by either depression (the severity of which varies), suicidal thoughts, feeling that you are not worth it, that life always serves rotten eggs and tomatoes or better still running away from the feeling by turning into addictive things like extreme music, drinking, smoking pot etc.

The trauma that people feel when their overtures towards these others (which may or may not be romantic Love, but just attempts to identify with the other) are met with rejection, feel the trauma at a much higher level as this is a highly emotional phase.

These may be attempts to fall in Love with the opposite or same sex, to make meaningful relationships with peers, to succeed in the new category of 'happening stuff' like playing the 'in' games, dressing up, etc.

Thus, depending on what happens to the freedom space of the heart chakra, the roads leading from here are either uphill or downhill.

The people whose root patterns are that their life is miserable and nothing good can happen to them lead the downhill path followed by those who are in relatively better patterns which may not go all the way down but settle for a compromised existence on the wayside.

The people going uphill definitely Love themselves and create a World where they are happy with the 'other'.

Grief

When we experience the emotion of being turned down by the one we Love, which can be conveyed as rejection, death, moving away of the Loved one or in other words abandonment from the Loved one, we experience grief.

It is a profound feeling of depression where one does not feel the need to survive at all. We have been abandoned so many times in life. And all the feelings of abandonment fill up a space within us that we tend to ignore or overlook. It is only when we touch grief again that all of the pain flows through.

One of the important things to remember while grieving is to grieve and allow all the pain to flow through. If there is grief, pause, look at it... and feel the pain. And it is perfectly ok to do so. Whatever else is important or taking up your mind space have to be kept aside at that point no matter what it is. And just grieve.

It is important to remember however, that grieving does not mean to indulge the thoughts of the grief. When you feel grief, grieve. Step aside from the thoughts as they make mountains out of molehills as they squirm their way through our minds. It does not help us. So pause the thoughts and just grieve.

Emptying the space which are holding the emotion of grief are very important for us to open up space for Love.

Forgiveness

One important fall out of the trauma is that people cling on to it and do not let go. (Yes, this is similar for trauma caused earlier, but the person here, is ready to understand the Wisdom of forgiveness).

Even though the person may not want to be hurt again and may try to numb himself, this is also a phase when they are willing to forgive. This comes in especially when there is a chance to forgive and forget the earlier trauma and move ahead with the same relationship (in such cases the forgiveness comes with a very selfish motive and is just about forgiving the person in the now as long as the same trauma is not repeated) or when the person understands that by not forgiving, he or she is holding onto the past and not allowing the present in.

Forgiving is never about the other person. True forgiving happens only when one understands what the 'non-forgiving' part is doing to us. When we do not forgive a person, we tend to keep going back in time to the same memory and the thoughts build up into a negative chaotic mass. And this weighs us down in our present. It is not only the moments we are thinking about the persons, but also generally the weight of the thought impacts how we are.

Also, by understanding that no one can undo the past and that it remains the way we remember it, etched in our memories. So, when we think of the cases where we have regrets and continue to have guilt, and by applying the Wisdom of guilt being a lie, we can also understand that the persons we are unable to forgive, would not have done it again today if they had our understanding of the situation.

By not forgiving a person, we do not affect the person at all. Please pay attention as this is a very important Wisdom. Each person has his or her own views about a particular situation. The theme is not common at all. Even within a household, each situation affects everyone in various ways. This can be understood through family constellations. But more on that soon. So, when every person has his or her view about a particular incident and we also realise that each person way of responding is majorly controlled by the patterns he or she has, we also understand that our 'not forgiving' will impact them only if they are ready to take on guilt as a way of response. And that too is not in our control.

Now, having understood this, do you feel forgiveness can impact anyone else other than you?

Imagine how it would feel to know that the person you are not willing to forgive is out there not aware of your emotions and generally enjoying life or going about life totally oblivious to your condition?

So, forgive... Let go... It relieves you of a burden.

In fact, the beauty of one of the methods of asking for forgiveness called 'Ho-pono-pono' tells us to ask for forgiveness of all the known, unknown things we may have done due to which we stand where we are and are going through the current situation. Similar is the emotion behind the Divine method of forgiveness called 'Micchami Dukkadam' practiced by the Jains in India.

Family constellations

Family constellations is a method used today to help us understand the varying energies that come together in each relationship and to understand how these affect us and can shift when we understand the underlying energies. This is a form of role play that helps us take on the roles in a particular situation without actually knowing anything about it. The energy is transferred from the person who is undergoing the issue and is Accepted unconditionally.

In this practice we must take up any one issue that we are facing in our lives and present it to the group. Post this we should think of the person in the actual situation in life and call on members who are willing to participate and in whom you see the energies associated with the actual person in real life. Then keeping your hands on the person's shoulders, transfer the energy of our perception of the person in the actual situation to him or her. We must do this even for a representation of our own self in the picture.

Now all the people whom we selected for this activity including the person who represents us are made to take positions in the space in the room as per whatever they feel intuitively. They are then made to express their views to the representative of us and the others in the group. Now we ask questions to the key players in the situation as per whatever we want to. They respond sensing the energies that they perceive.

While this entire exercise may seem like a game or a play, it is interesting to note that the person whose situation has been adapted to be played out is awe struck by what comes out of this play (ninety nine percent of the time). Just his transferring the energy to the people play acting the roles of the actual people in the situation makes them respond exactly like the actual people even if they have never met them!

The gist of what everyone understands at the end of the process is that everyone has his or her own priorities and reasons to be invested in any situation and that varies from person to person even when they are closely related.

It is important to let go of the energy within you when you step out of the process of family constellations. So, all the participants hold hands and let go of any energy that is not their own and re-call all their energies that they may have left with the people. Just using intention for this is enough.

Jealousy

This is a Powerful energy that can prevent our experiencing what True Love is.

The basic nature of this energy is possessiveness. So, it is related to the overall possessive nature of the person that originates in the root chakra. However, in the Heart chakra, it becomes about owning a person. It becomes about feeling insecure and territorial when another person seems to be getting closer to your friend / Lover or the other person is your friend / Lover and is showing attraction / affection to a third person or better still, your friend / Lover is perceived to be getting something more than what you have got.

Here, the interesting thing is that the very reason we feel jealousy is that we too have the same facet in us, however, we have ignored the same.

For example, if you feel the person who is getting attention or Love is due to their looks, you too have it, but are not attending to it. If you feel they have more money, you too have means to make similar money, but are not giving it too much attention. If you feel their attire is better, you haven't been giving to much attention to yours. Because there is nothing out there that can capture your attention unless you have already got it within you.

So, look at opportunities where jealousy comes your way as opportunities to look for those facets which are already present in you to develop them. It is the Universe's way of showing you.

Love

One of the most Divine experiences that we can ever have. But the Truth is to just understand that we ourselves are Love!

It is important to get rid of all the stuff that we believe we are and allow the True essence of Love to flow out of you. As mentioned earlier while discussing grief, we need to drain out all the grief so that Love can fill its space. And Love comes out of us – not the exterior. Similarly look at all the other things that have taken the space that originally was meant for Love.

Attention seeking, anger, jealousy and most importantly the external ego have no space within you if you genuinely seek Love. So, Observe them and you know how to let them go...

We have to allow this flow of Love to fill us first and then allow it to seep outwards into the World.

Become Love

How do you become Love?

Choose only those things which you Love in life no matter what. Choose those options which make you feel valued. Choose to move apart from people and things that do not respond to your Love and do not cling to them. It is important as what you are experiencing in relationships where you do not feel valued is not Love.

Perhaps if you move away, you will also experience the very thing you are trying hard for – to be Loved. Try it...

The energy of Love is very profound. It is subtle yet very Powerful. One doesn't even realise how it works but one is compelled by it. It is not the Love of a particular physique or a face or a flower. It is Love itself. It has the capacity to attract anything in front of it. It is full by itself, and you can only create fullness from it.

It begins with self-Love. And this is a Conscious effort to only Love your own self. Which means allow yourself to only experience that which you are clear is leading to something amazing that you have always wanted. It begins with the smallest of things. Choosing things in daily life because you Truly want it – not because someone else likes it or that it what is expected of you.

When you Truly become Love, you recognise that it is True that you are the centre of the Universe and the Universe is just playing parts to make every wish of yours True. Manifestation becomes faster.

The Powerful thing about Love is that once you get into this habit, the Universe conspires to bring to you only that which is awesome in your eyes. This is called the Power of Reflections

Reflections

This too is one of the Powerful Wisdoms in this journey. And this remains a concept and not reality in people who do not genuinely move into the Heart chakra. So, beware – You may see this as profound Wisdom or utter nonsense and not 'live'it...

Yes, this is real!

When one Truly transcends the idea that there are 'others' in this Universe, different from ourselves, we reach this realm of the Heart.

We only touch this space when we stop complaining about 'others', the Universe, circumstances etc. And this cannot be done as a self-regulation alone. It comes from the understanding that whatever we do to anybody or anything outside of us, the emotion it generates hits us back somewhere.

This was also the concept on which Karma was based. However, there is a difference. In Karma everything you do or have done in the past creates a similar energy in the present and future which you will have to face. However, in the case of Reflections, everything is in the present. Everything we are doing in the present moment or present time reflects back to us.

There is no more past!

Pay attention now! Any disturbance we sense from the centre or our sense of wellbeing, it could be an emotion or a thought or an action or words we sense in another person is somewhere being done by us in the present moment. There are no exceptions to this rule ever!

So, if you feel you are being ridiculed by your boss or being triggered by your in-laws, pause, you are doing the same to someone else right now. The words may not be the same, the sensed emotion may not be the same, but there is someone out there receiving the exact same energy from you right now!

So, what can we do to correct this?

Pause and remember where you are doing it. When you realise this just set an intent never to do the same again. Do this from the understanding that you are creating the World you are experiencing. So, anything that you do comes back to you instantly.

If you begin to see this, you are advancing towards the time you realise that the entire Universe is just your Reflection. Enjoy the ride!

The Thymus gland

The Thymus gland secretes Thymosin that is essential in the creation of the T-cells that build up our immunity.

It is similar to the Love that flows towards us and so makes us more capable of withstanding any kind of infection or disease. The Love energy energizes the Thymus and so creates more of Thymosin.

This connection between our immunity and Love is the energy output of the Heart chakra.

Any issues in the Thymosin production can be corrected by bring in the Love energy towards everyone.

Opening your Heart chakra by hugging

One easy and important way to make changes to existing relationships and new ones is to learn to hug the person with whom the relationship is not going that well.

For instance, if you are having problems with your father that you want to resolve, start by hugging him everyday for two full minutes. Yes, two full minutes! Yes, it may be too much of an effort initially. But it has to be done.

And do it regularly for twenty-one days (Twenty-one days is the time taken to form new neuronal pathways in your brain).

And there is a right method of hugging. Stand firmly on both feet with feet slightly apart and face the other person. Look the person in the eye with a gentle smile on your lips. Look into both eyes. What you see in the eye is the Soul. Now hug the person straight with your heart holding them straight in your open arm and stroking their back with one hand and holding the person with the other. This stroking should be done in concentric circles around the Heart chakra on his or her spine. Hold this position for two minutes.

You are awesome!

Meditation on the Heart chakra

Sit with an erect spine and your legs folded. Place your hands in your lap facing upwards. Close your eyes. Observe your breath for a few minutes. Then take the attention to the body parts which are calling out to you. Spend time with each of them saying "I am with you" and mean it. Repeat this till the disturbance moves away. Pay attention to your breath again.

Slowly bring your awareness to the Heart Chakra. With each breath also become aware of the pulsation of your Heart. Lab-dab lab-dab lab-dab. It has been doing it from the womb and has never ever let you down. Isn't it something to be Grateful for? Fill your Heart with Gratitude and allow it to radiate out of you out into the Universe and back into you through the back of your Heart. Welcome it in. Allow this cycle of Gratitude to flow out from the front and back into your Heart from the behind to continue for a few minutes.

Now imagine that you are seated in your most favourite outdoor space. Feel the radiance of the Sun shining down on you. Feel the breeze. Hear the sound of the birds. Hear the water flowing. Feel the completeness in the picture with you in the centre. Send out Love to every part of this picture, be it the place you are seated, the winds, the trees, the flowing river, the Sun, all of it. Now feel each of them returning the Love to you. Feel the waves of Love flowing back into your Heart through the back of your Heart chakra. Receive it with Gratitude. Allow this cycle of Love to flow in and out of your body. Feel it circulate even within your body through the blood. Feel it flow to every nook and cranny within your body. And finally flow out of you to the beautiful space you are in.

Whenever you want to bring in somebody with whom you want the relationship to improve, imagine them sitting in front of you. Send them Love from the front of your Heart chakra to the back of theirs. After a little while you will sense them filling up with the Love and sending you back Love. Receive it through the back of your Heart chakra.

Centre in this wonderful feeling of being the centre of Love.

When you feel complete, rub your palms and place them over your eyes. Gently move your fingers and toes and then gently open your eyes.

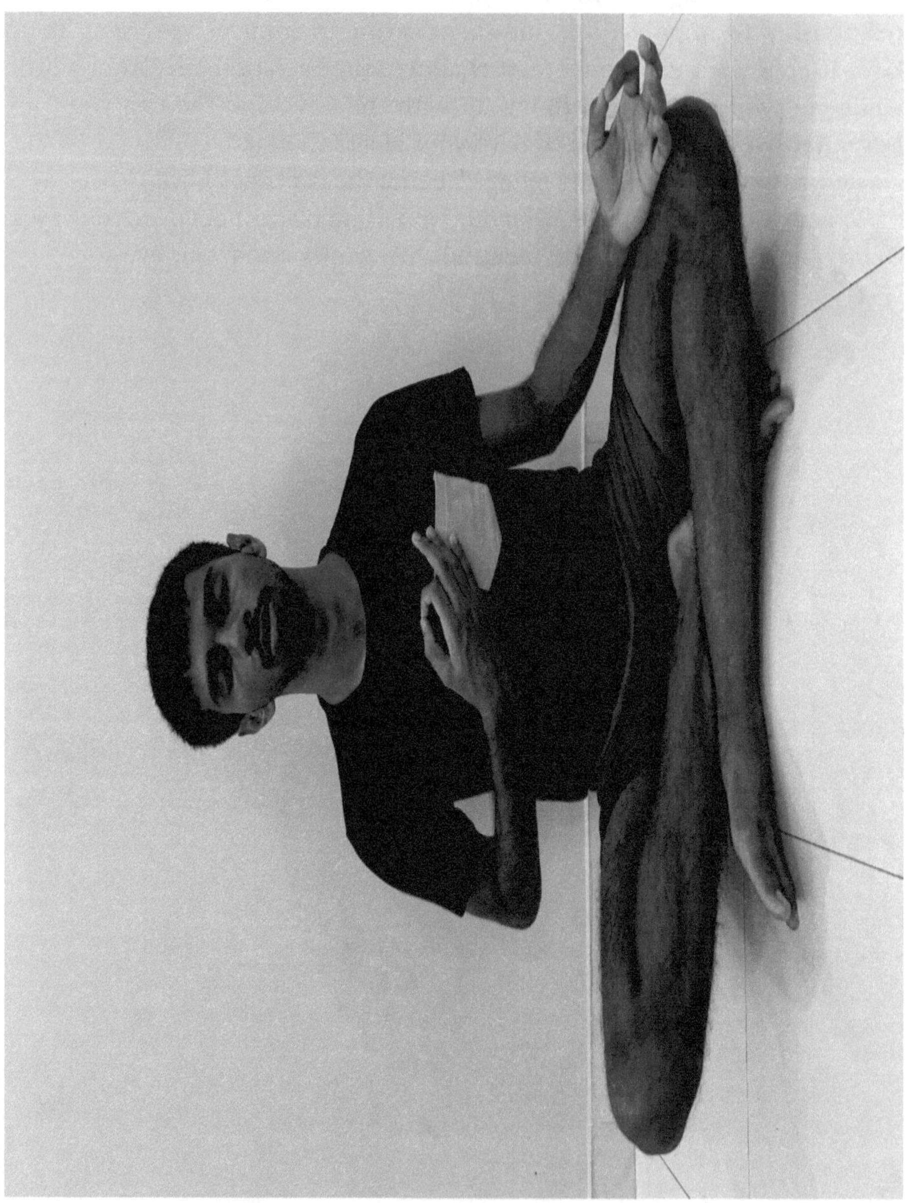

Fig 10: The hand positions (mudra) for the Anahata Chakra

Wisdom of the Heart Chakra

1. The Heart opens a new way of being. The realisation of there is no 'other'
2. You have to be Love to perceive receiving Love from anyone. So be Love
3. Remove all the elements within you that do not allow you to become Love like grief, jealousy, anger etc.
4. Experience Reflections
5. Resonate with Love
6. Be Love

CHAPTER SIX

The Vishuddhi Chakra – The Communication centre

The better-known facts

The Vishuddhi chakra or the energy centre that fosters Purity is placed along the spine in the region of the neck. It is a sixteen petalled flower, light blue in colour, with two sides, one facing the inside of the body from the spine and the other facing out of the body – behind.

This chakra has the energy of ether – the space that holds all of us in place. It fills all the spaces between everything we see from the largest stars and galaxies to each cell and each atom within us.

This is again a masculine chakra. Interestingly it is the masculine version of creativity that was born in the Sacral chakra. It is the expressive part of the same.

It is the seat of communication. The space where we feel the connectedness to communicate what we feel, why and how.

The seeds syllable or mantra for this Chakra is "Ham" chanted in the G-scale. It is chanted by keeping the fingers of both hands inter-twined within and the thumbs touching and placed close to the Throat.

All the nerves of the body are governed by the Throat chakra. It deals with speech.

It deals with all issues related to the Throat chakra like chronic laryngitis, hoarse throat, skin disorders, Thyroid problems, mouth ulcers etc.

A balanced throat chakra reflects in a person being well adjusted and totally non-judgemental about the World around him or her.

Fig 11: Vishuddhi Chakra

Lesser-known facts

Experiences during this phase

This stage is post-puberty and the stage when one comes out of the 'crush' phase of the Heart and the intense feelings of Love for the 'other'.

This is the phase when the need to be Truthful to the other comes up and the person decides to express himself or herself fully to the other. This is about showing the person our inner self and being True.

All the things that we took for granted are questioned. All the comforts and problems of home are broken out of. The person sets out into the World to prove to himself or herself and to the other what he or she is Truly about.

It is interesting that the self comes to realise that we are not always Truthful. We Choose to create a splendorous World out there for the others to see (as per whatever each person's Choice is). This covers or hides another side visible only to the select few who are close enough. And finally, there are a lot of intimate secrets that tie us down. And this phase is about destroying all the walls in between.

Later on, the self also realises that there are sides of himself or herself that are not known to himself or herself. These may be things visible to the external person or may again be hidden by closed walls. There are sides unknown to us which may not be visible to anyone at all! And so, the person now Chooses to break these walls. The person Chooses to discover himself or herself.

It is when the self is standing naked in front of another and is comfortable with it that this phase is complete and the Throat chakra is completely open.

Communication

There are things which have to be exchanged between people beyond the material exchanges. These are thoughts and concepts in verbal form or written or painted or art forms. There is a meaning to each stance, each mudra, each intonation that is understood by the person who is receiving the communication either fully or partially. This is communication.

Communication can be verbal, through poetry, writing or actual words spoken or through dance, music, drawing, painting, or any other fine arts.

In daily communication, there are conversations that may be good or not good depending on what they elicit as a response in either of the conversationalists or in someone watching the scene.

This difference in the perception of each individual based on the patterns they are born with, their understanding of the situation, their biases and non-biases, the associations they have given to the words being used create the meanings in their minds.

So, it is not necessary at all that two person who are involved in a particular conversation are understanding it the same way. There are bound to be differences and these differences cause different experiences.

Hence the saying that there is a right time and place for any idea to be communicated for it to be effective. If all the energies are right, the effect will be what one perceives as expected.

However, clearing this Chakra makes this easier. Conversations will be successful when the throat chakra is cleared. The person will be able to express his or her Truth easily.

Truth

What is the Truth? It is what is perceived as a correct thing as opposed to something that is perceived as a lie? Who decides it? Is there a Universal Truth? How is it perceived?

Interesting questions!

People may state that the Sun rising in the east is a Truth that cannot have a lie in it. Doesn't that depend on where one is located in the Universe? For example what would it be for someone inside the Sun? What if one is watching the Sun from any of the planets or comets outside this solar system? Doesn't it make the Sun move from West to East and North to South and South to North as well?

So, Truth is relative. And Truth can only be verified and ascertained a Truth by someone who is reliable. Who is reliable and who judges the reliability? For instance, can we say that the judges in court are reliable? They may be, but are they hundred percent of the time?

So then what is a Universal Truth?

From where we stand, the only Universal Truths are those which cannot be questioned by the Universe itself. Everything else is a perception which has at least two sides to it.

People just perceive the Truth

Perception

As mentioned earlier, perception is a product of the patterns, the mood, the things the person is paying attention to and the beliefs of a person. Perhaps more than that. The point is it is only what which is perceived which comes into the consideration set of things which then are considered to bring out the Truth of the person in the moment.

For instance, the person could be someone who is used to searching for what is wrong in his surrounding and so perceives the filth around him and hears whatever is wrong with the people around. He may be more wary and suspicious of his neighbours and so may perceive a new neighbour to be of suspicious character. As he believes this, he sees proof of what he is looking for in the way the new neighbour behaves and so perceives him to be untrustworthy.

Or, if a person believes that her religion is superior to others, she sees proof in the way things work out better only for her folk. As she is looking for this as proof, she ignores the things to the contrary and only picks up the information that supports it – all unknowingly of course.

If perception is so singular and individualised, what is the Truth?

Reality

Reality is what is in any given point of time and place. Remember, this is devoid of any additional thoughts or emotions. So, a person being at a place at a given time is real. However, what he or she sees or hears is subjective and only perceived.

What is real can be seen by everyone or felt by everyone or heard by everyone at that point of time. Period!

Everything beyond is perceived.

Today the temperature is 28 degrees Celsius at 8:10 PM in a particular spot in a particular road, in Kochi, Kerala. Everything beyond this like, 'it is hot', 'it is sultry' are perceptions. They differ from person to person.

The Truth of the Throat chakra makes us open to these realities and takes us away from our personalised perceptions.

Our reality

We are a sum total of everything that we perceive in the Universe. So, if we perceive persecution, or terrorism, or murder to philandering in the Universe, it is because we too have it within us.

This is taking the energy of Reflections in the Heart chakra one step forward. Everything we perceive in the World is definitely alive in us!

We are the rapist, the killer, the manipulator that we read about. When we let go of these energies in our daily lives, they disappear from our perceptions.

So, most of you may tell me at this point, 'I am not at all a rapist – I respect women' or 'I am not a murderer'. Are you really not?

Anything we believe in, tend to think about or act out on are all things we have to take responsibility for. For example, when we are reacting to thoughts of a murder, we may be strangling the murderer in our minds or raping women in our dreams. All this indicates that those energies are alive within us. And remember, we Truly do not know ourselves. We only understand ourselves in the confines of the energies we live with every day. We have not explored what will happen should one of the essential energies' change.

This becomes clearer in our head when we try to understand why certain people who seem normal otherwise take extreme steps when they are forced to beyond what they themselves thought possible. This could be strangling a tiger or killing a person.

So, we are all walking talking prostitutes, pimps, perverts, racists, rapists, manipulators etc. Do not run away from this. Face it. Accept it. It is a huge relief when we see it all in us. Because, when we Truly do, we also have the Power to make it go away. We only need to correct our beliefs.

We only need to believe that it is quite ok being all of these. And to let go of the energies of those we do not want in our lives. For example, for rape to go away, I just need to work on my own energies of violating people in their personal spaces. When I Truly let go of that, my World will be a much more beautiful space.

Similarly, all the negative adjectives given above have a meaning which will make us Accept them. For example, terrorising could mean making another feel threatened by our presence. And, racists could mean feeling too much Love for your own people. And a prostitute could mean being willing to give up your values to get something in return.

Isn't the World already seeming nicer?

Manifestation

We create the World we see around us. Every single element of what you see around is created by you!

Yes, we have created our experiences out of nothing by the thoughts we think and the words we speak. Every thought is the raw material of something we want to create out there. It becomes even more Powerful when we think about it over and over again. It becomes most Powerful when we speak about it. But the actual ingredient to manifestation is the emotion of knowing it is done. When we believe it is done - it is!

You would have noticed that most of what you are experiencing in life right now has taken time to manifest. And they are not exactly the way you would have 'wished them' to be. That is because of the myriad of thoughts and emotions that have come over the original thought that confused the Universe on what it is exactly that you are looking for.

Yes, even the horrible things that have happened in your life have been manifested by the most Powerful person in the Universe – You! The thoughts may not exactly be that you are going to be mugged or raped.

However, there is fear, there is insecurity. And these build up to create the exact thing that you manifested. Difficult that it is to take responsibility for this, pause and think – Isn't it True?

Thyroid gland

The Thyroid gland secretes Thyroxine that regulates the metabolism in the body and balances the salts in the blood. This is again a direct relation to the way the Truth enhances the balancing views of ours on any situation. It brings about equilibrium in the person.

Any issues related to Thyroxine or para-thyroxine production in our body can be corrected by just ensuring that we are always in Truth.

Exercises to strengthen the Throat Chakra

Focus on creativity. Draw, paint, sing, play an instrument, sculpt or create pottery, speak extempore. Any of these practices done regularly can ease out the Throat chakra. It is important to keep all of these in a creative space. For example, it is important not to just follow what has already been done. Allow the creative juices to flow and allow these to come out of you the way your inner self wants them to.

Even chanting a mantra regularly opens the Throat chakra. Choose any mantra (preferably a long one) and recite them regularly.

Throat chakra meditation

Sit down in a quiet space with your spine erect. Close your eyes and focus on your breath. Take your attention to spaces within you that call out for your attention. Say 'I am with you' and mean it and be with those spaces till they settle down.

Observe your breath. Observe how each breath feels as it moves in and out of you. When you Observe your mind wandering, pause and bring it back to the breath non-judgementally.

When you have settled down completely and your mind is empty, focus on any one topic that comes spontaneously to mind and allow yourself to speak about it. Do not control the words or sentences. Just listen to whatever is being spoken about. Do it till you have expressed whatever it is that you want to. This is when you feel complete. Thank the Divine and slowly rub your palms. Place them over your eyes and gently open your eyes.

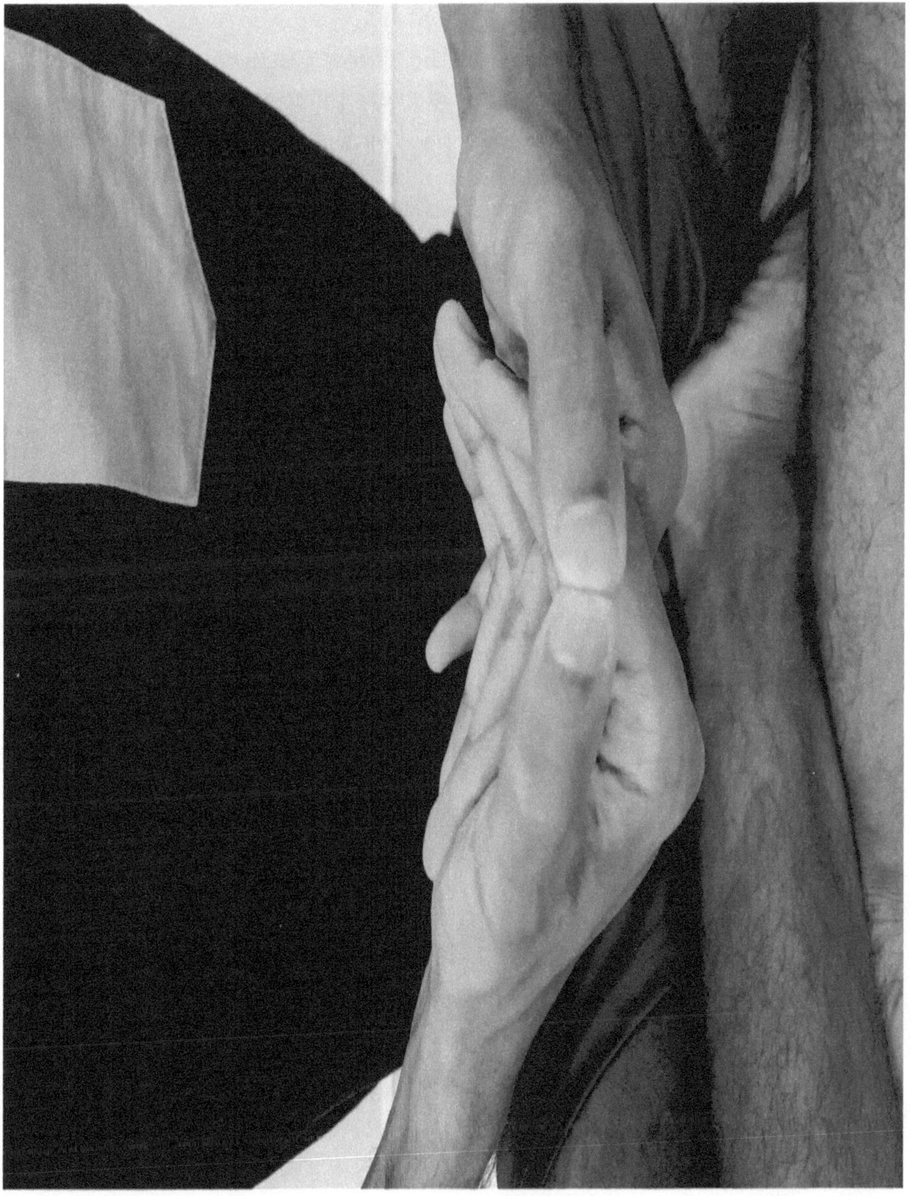

Fig 12: The hand position (mudra) for the Vishuddhi Chakra

Wisdom of the Throat chakra

1. The importance of Truth comes in the Throat Chakra
2. Truth is relative and is dependent on every person's Perception
3. The ability to manifest whatever we think, speak and feel with emotions comes in this Chakra
4. We can create the perfect World we want if we clear all the things that we feel are negative from our own selves

CHAPTER SEVEN

The Ajna Chakra – The Control centre

Rudra Granthi

This is the veil of delusion that has to be removed for our Consciousness to reside in the Ajna or above. And the delusion is of our non-Acceptance of our Divine nature. This part of the chakra system is also called the Super-Conscious part of it.

It is only when we Truly Accept that we too are Divine that we have access to the Wisdom stored in the Ajna.

If the Divine is indeed Omnipresent, isn't it egoistic to think we are not part of the Divine and hence the Divine does not exist in us? ?

Yes, we are Divine!

The better-known facts

The Ajna or the Third eye chakra is located between the eyebrows slightly above it and is visualized as a two petal flower points outwards from the middle of the forehead and a similar flower pointing backwards from the posterior fontanelle or the slight depression on the posterior side of the cranium. It is the penultimate chakra and governs the activity of all the other chakras (controlling them)

It is the feminine of the Power chakra in the Solar Plexus. It is the centre of intuition and our supernatural Powers (yes, we do have an area which corresponds to supernatural Powers which can be honed for us to exhibit them).

The flower petals of the Ajna are actually composed of many petals arranged to make them seem like one larger petal in each of the two petals. The colour of the Ajna is indigo. The element associated with the Ajna is sound.

The endocrine gland associated with the Ajna chakra is the pituitary gland (also known as the master gland in the body which regulated the flow of hormones from all the other endocrine glands).

The Ajna chakra activation happens by chanting the mantra "Om" in A-scale. The mudra or hand position to be held during the chant is to touch both the thumbs upper portion facing inwards, the nails of the index fingers touching each other in an inverted position and the remaining three fingers pointing outwards and touching each other at the tips.

The entry of Consciousness into this chakra is restricted by the Rudra Granthi.

Fig 13: The Ajna Chakra (Third eye chakra)

Lesser-known facts

The Ajna or Third eye is the centre where both the Pingala and the Ida naadis meet for the last time. Beyond this is the space of oneness. It is the area where we conquer all the masculine and feminine polarities and settle down into oneness. It is the non-judgemental space where everything is Accepted as is.

It is the beginning of the space where we realise that we are supernatural too!

In fact, there are eight 'siddhis' that have been identified in the Hindu Wisdom which are supposed to open up on their own when our third eye gets activated. They are:

Anima – the Power to Choose to become tinier than what we are

Mahima – the Power to Choose to become larger than what we are

Laghima – the Power to Choose to become lighter than what we are

Garima – the Power to Choose to become heavier than what we are

Prapti – the Power to Choose to be anywhere in this Universe instantly

Prakamya – the Power to manifest whatever it is that we desire

Ishita – the Power to control nature & beings

Vashita – the Power to attract anything in nature

However, these as already explained are side effects of the journey. They should not be the end of the journey in our heads as then our ego engages with these Powers. And this can derail us from our journey to the Crown.

Hence, should you experience these, just enjoy them, do not get attached to them or to what we enjoy about them.

This phase is also about concentration, intuition, non-judgement, sleep, dreams etc. So, now more about them

Concentration

This chakra is about the lower brain and all the nerves in our body. However, this chakra is also about Concentration. When this chakra is optimal in its functioning the concentration Powers are enhanced and the person is able to focus on any given activity well.

Concentration is accompanied by the pressure in the eyebrow area and frowning for most people when it is not easy to concentrate. When the Third eye is open or active optimally, this comes easily to us. All the nerves are functioning optimally and so there is no need to apply any external pressure.

When the chakra is sub-optimal in performance the traits exhibited becomes distraction or in-attention.

Intuition

Intuition is the very first thought or feeling that imprints in a clear mind that is not born from any previous thought. It is something that is placed in the clear space of the mind by the higher self. When we learn to understand intuitions, it gives us clarity as messages which are always true.

Now, for an important point. Every one of us is intuitive. We have just lost the faculty due to the overload of thoughts and patterns in our mind. We have forgotten to recognise the first thought that comes in without any previous thought about it on its own. Practicing watching and understanding intuitive thoughts can help to build up the strength of the same.

There are numerous ways that we can build up intuitions. I am suggesting one way to get started. Call in a partner who also wants to try this. Sit facing each other with eyes closed and legs folded. Focus your attention on the third eye of your partner and send out a word as a thought, an emotion, an image and a sound in your mind (not aloud). Hold this for about fifteen seconds. Ask the person to guess what it was. The answer may not be direct. For example, the person may only pick up that it was a red coloured object when you were thinking of an apple. So, allow for anything that the person had picked up to be expressed. Once the person has finished expressing, tell him exactly what you thought, the word, the emotion, the image, the sound. Do this for around five rounds each. See what the success percentage was. Keep practicing everyday till the percentage improves and you are able to intuit whatever your friend is thinking.

We can take this example out into the world and try to find answers to questions you do not know about.

Overtime, you can build up your intuition to see the answers to just about anything in this World. Yes, they will all be True.

Sleep

The Third eye is also the Chakra which looks after the unconscious state of sleep which includes the state where the person is totally unconscious (deep sleep) and the state where he or she is alternately conscious state of dreams.

For now, we will look at the deeply unconscious state of sleep. This is a normal phase that precedes the dream state. It is generally divided into 3 parts by the scientific community. It is called NREM sleep or non-rapid eye movement sleep. This phase is repeated multiple times every night when people sleep. This phase largely helps in relaxing the person every night and it is important for the time spent in these phases every night.

People with chakra disturbances in the Ajna may suffer sleeplessness or oversleep. The lack of sleep does not allow the complete relaxation of the person. Overtime this builds up and clear complications in the persons life even on a mental level. This too can be balanced by balancing the chakra or activating it if it is not done.

Sleep is caused when the para-sympathetic nervous system takes over in the circadian rhythm. This means that every day, there is a cycle in which the sympathetic nervous system and para-sympathetic nervous system alternately and this happens in a given time frame. The sympathetic nervous system is at its peak at 3-4 PM and the para-sympathetic nervous peaks at around 3-4 AM. When the para-sympathetic nervous system peaks, it brings about tiredness, sleepiness etc. So, enhancing para-sympathetic nervous system brings about sleep. People with sleeping disorders need to bring out the para-sympathetic effects in them.

Breathing through the left nostril brings up the para-sympathetic stimulation within the body and cools and quietens the body. People suffering from sleeplessness need to breathe through their left nostril for 5-10 mins and then sleep turning towards their left side.

In addition, they are to avoid bright lights or radiations from devices at least an hour before sleep.

Overtime as one chants the 'Om' mantra, the chakra balances out and the sleep cycles are restored.

Dreams

In the remaining phases of sleep there are rapid eye movements (REM sleep) which are because of the dreams being seen by the person. Rapid eye movement sleep is the last phase of the sleep cycle, and the level of Consciousness is just before waking up. However, one goes through REM sleep also many times in a night and we see multiple dreams in each REM phase. Only the memory of those dreams are retained that are seen just before waking up.

Dreams are the method by which nature or the Universe converses with us. It gives us clues as to what we are doing (most people are so engrossed in their lives that they forget what they are doing) and also gives us options to consider and shows us new openings. To understand this, we must also understand the meaning of dreams.

Every dream that we see is just a visual aspect of the different parts of us. There is a part (in most cases) of the Observer in the dream and the people and things around him. Each of the people and things in the dream represent as aspect of the person itself. For example, if the person sees himself waking up in the old house of his (which in reality is not the case) and sees his dear relative dead, it means that he has accessed an old part of him and now the dear part of him (which can be better explained with adjectives like Loving, caring etc) is 'dead' that was alive at that point in time.

Another example is the dream of a person missing the bus regularly. This points to the fact that the person has anxiety about being able to complete the tasks at hand.

If one is able to pay attention to dreams regularly and act on whatever it is that the Universe is trying to tell you, we are sorted. There are no terrible dreams or nightmares if we understand the True meaning of the dreams.

Beings

People who are prone to see other beings which are not from this dimension where we think we exist have a Third eye that is definitely more active than others. This is not to say that all things that move in the dark are ghosts.

Yes, there are other beings beyond what we feel there are as per the zoology and botany textbooks. There are beings beyond the realm of what we are used to seeing. Taking it further, there are beings which are entirely in the ultraviolet and infrared spectrums and hence are not visible to us. There are also beings in realms which we do not have access to or have partial access to.

Getting in touch with such beings is an experience that comes through when the third eye is open or active. We get used to the concept, then the presence and then if you hone it, even communication with these beings.

Let's talk about 'ghosts'. The concept of ghosts is True. When I say it is True, it only means that the conventional notion of a person's energies staying back at the time of his death and beyond is True.

Let me explain this further. When we enter certain rooms or meet certain people, we become aware of the emotions in the room or the emotions of the person even though a word may not be exchanged. And if this person is a depressed person, the depression stays in the room long after the person leaves. It is more prominent around the places the person touched or was close to. This is the energy body of the person.

Similarly, when a person dies, he or she has attachments to this realm. Some of it may be so strong that he she may Choose to leave behind that energy aspect here. In severely Traumatic cases, this energy body may have a 'life of its own'. So, you hear about ghosts that walk down a staircase every day at midnight or a child ghost who keeps looking out of a window. It is not as if these ghosts do not have any other work, it is just that they are only capable of that. They do not have the faculty of a fully alive person. They can only do the action that is attributed to them.

And not all ghosts are dangerous. Most are so passive and neutral; we do not even notice them. They cling onto people who have the 'victim' energy. They also enter people who have the qualities they are looking for. For example, a ghost that wants to enjoy eating will enjoy it passively by entering a person who will then show cravings for a particular type of food. The dangerous ones are not even half as dangerous as they are made out to be. They may be traumatised by the way they lost their life and so want to change their life story. So, they keep appearing in the same space over and over again. Similar to our inner children.

Judgement

The Ajna is the final frontier before the Sahasrara. It is only till here that the Kundalini can rise. Here it has to wait for the Divine. And this is the space where the two polarities within the body - the masculine and the feminine meet. So, in this space there is no gender once the Chakra is awakened. It is the union of both the genders.

We experience this is daily life as the merging of the polarities within us.

What I mean by the merging of the polarities is that we may have a strong opinion about something where we are not open to the other viewpoint. This may be over reasons like religion and caste or even trivial ones like the kind of friends you 'Accept'. There is clearly an opposing polarity there which could be someone subscribing to a philosophy which is the opposite of this. Merging of the polarity means that the aspect which is causing the 'opinion' ceases to exist in our heads. It really doesn't matter whether this polarity exists or does not exist. It is just there. There are no opinions on the same. It is just a neutral element.

The entire exercise in the Ajna chakra is to reach this stage for every single thing. See it without judgement. Yes, Love it to. And Accept it Lovingly.

The Eternal Life

This is also the stage when one becomes aware that one is eternal! The concept of birth and death and just the punctuations in our journey. We have always existed. Yes, we can help this experience by meditation by taking the person to the previous and later lives in this linear aspect of our understanding. However, the Truth of it all sinks in. The fear of death vanishes. The fear of abandonment is no more. One becomes aware that one is just a Divine light that is experiencing this journey called life in this realm. There is a lot more, a great lot more...

However, before this Truly awakens in our journey, the fears of the unknown things done in the past births brings about the accentuating of the Karma in our lives. This is also a phase when the karmas come back to play a role in the persons life. This may cause the person to explore past lives and thus come to terms with his or her existence in a past life unknown till then to him or her. The experiences post the exploration help to consolidate the Wisdom by seeing the similarities and the new knowledge and the effects of the same in this life.

Facing death also becomes just another experience where the person begins to see it for what it is – an interim punctuation mark.

Trataka meditation

The third eye can be activated by performing the Trataka kriya or the Trataka meditation regularly. For this you need to sit in a dark room facing a lit candle. The candle needs to be placed at chest level with the flame at the eye level. Stare at the candle and try not to blink your eyes 10-15 seconds. Now close your eyes and hold the vision of the flame in your third eye for as long as you can see it. Do not strain to see it.

Repeat this exercise at least 3 times. Work on seeing the flame inside for 4X times. As we go along, we can increase the initial staring of the raw flame for a minute and focus on the inner flame for 4 minutes.

This helps to build up the eye muscles and also strengthens the Third eye and its faculties.

Meditating on the Third eye chakra

Sit calmly in an erect posture with folded legs and eyes closed. Observe your thoughts unconditionally. Just allow them to dissipate as we Observe them.

Now take your attention to the body parts that are calling out to you. For each part bring your attention to it and say, "I am with you" and mean it and be with it till it relaxes.

Now Observe your breath. Observe the air as it moves in and out of your body. After a few minutes, take your attention to your third eye. Imagine the eye opening up (See an eyelid moving apart) and see the eye being able to see.

Allow your attention to drift towards what the third eye sees. At this juncture you can even put up a question to the Third eye that you want an answer to.

Now allow whatever comes up to reveal itself to you. Just Observe that we do not engage with the visuals. Just see and capture everything that we remember of the scene. When you feel complete, come out of the meditation and journal it.

Repeat this exercise every day

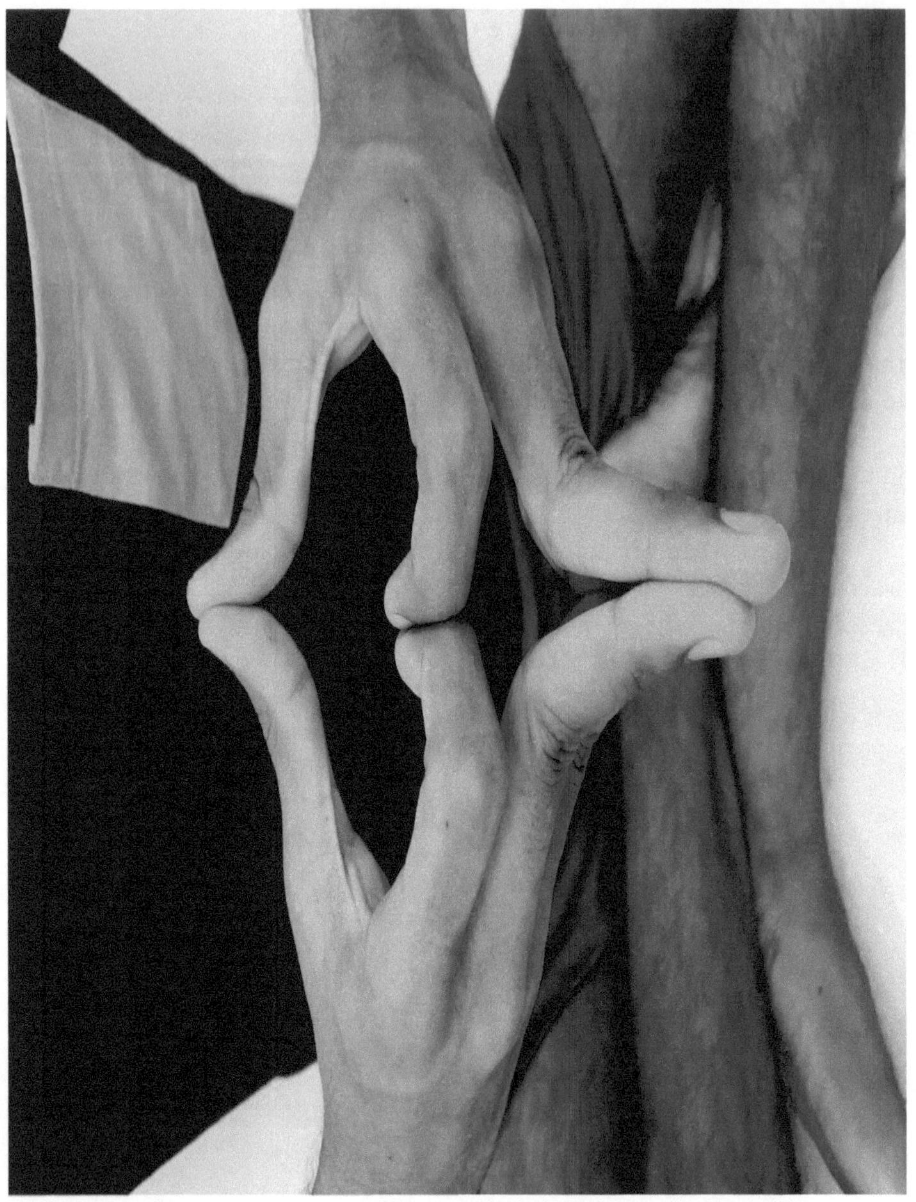

Fig 14: The hand postion (mudra) for the Ajna Chakra

Wisdom of the Third eye

1. Judgements are just our ego's views. Do not judge
2. Be open to intuitions
3. Listen to the messages from your dreams. They will guide you
4. Accept everything that the Universe puts in front of you
5. Be focussed on the Divine

CHAPTER EIGHT

The Sahasrara Chakra – Meeting the Divine

The final frontier! The last major chakra that is partly in the human energy and mostly Divine. This is the final step of the journey where you resonate with Oneness!

Better known facts

This is the thousand petalled lotus that spins the fastest and it the most subtle of all chakras. It is seen as violet in colour that transforms to white and then to gold. Some people also see it as a mix of the rainbow colours.

This chakra has only one face, pointing up to father sky from the top of our skull. It is an inch above the skull area.

You can activate this chakra by chanting Mmm... or Om with your mouth closed and with your palms jointed and your fingers clasping the other hand with only you two little fingers raised and touching each other. This mudra has to be placed above your head. The chant has to be done in the B-scale.

The element that rules this chakra is Light. And as already mentioned, as it points towards father sky, it is a totally masculine chakra – the Divine masculine.

The chakra governs all the higher faculties of the brain and controls both the cerebral hemispheres. In fact, it is here that the Divine waits for us (Yes, we do not have to wait for the Divine. The Divine is forever present). It waits for us to be fully ready. And when we are, we send out the signals to the "Brahmarandra" or cave of the Brahman which is an empty space within the brain where the Ida and Pingala finally meet. It is the cranial cavity in the head. There is a secretion of a particular liquid into this cavity once the Ida and Pingale unite. This sends out vibrations of the completion of the human part of the journey. At least as far as the meeting of the two polarities are concerned.

The remaining step happens when another liquid is secreted by the Pineal gland within the crevice of the cerebrum above the cerebellum and above the Pituitary gland as well into the same cavity or the Brahmarandra. This happens when the yearning from the human crosses over to the realisation that what is being yearned for by us is also what is yearning for us...

When both these liquids mix in this cavity and fill it, it causes an explosion in the nerve endings as all the nerve endings within the brain fire simultaneously. And the human brain of which most of us use only three to four percent is catapulted to a 100% active nature where all of it is alive.

This is Enlightenment. This is the stage when our awareness is completely alive!

As the location specifies, this Chakra is about the central nervous system, the cerebrum in particular, the top of the spinal cord and associated nerves.

The common issues faced by people whose Sahasrara is not fully open or active are frustration, illusions, depression, joylessness, destructive feelings, headaches, Spiritual addiction and Spiritual aversion, detachment from the body.

The reason we experience all these including depression and illusions is because we are separated from the Divine or too involved with the Divine connection. We may indulge our visions of this World and the way it seems to us too much and become too separated from reality as seen by others and so have illusions. We may separate ourselves from the Divine when our chakra is closed and lose hope in ever being connected to the ever-present Divine and so suffer depression. All the other examples are just lesser versions of these two.

The balanced Sahasrara exhibits as people Joyous in the moment and feeling connected to the Divine and hance to everything around. All the senses are working optimally, and all the faculties are flowering.

Fig 15: The Sahasraar Chakra (Crown)

Lesser-known facts (Err... Well... If you want to know, you do)

What is 'God'?

I hope everyone will agree with the following things

God is everywhere (Omnipresence) – So, He or She is within us too... And He or She is within everyone else too (Including the conniving prude of a person who is standing opposite you ?) So, if everything and everyone is God, and we Truly believe it... then how would we express ourselves to God? How would we receive anything from anybody outside keeping in mind that the thing received is being received from God, by God! May be either of you or both of you, or one of you is not aware...

God can create any miracle at any point in time (Omni-potency) including that miracle that you have been telling yourself can never happen, or can happen only for others, or will take a very long time to happen, or you have lost the chance in this time for it to happen again... If not, He or She is not God!

God can intervene at any time – if you are willing ?. Yes... only if you are willing... Remember, it is we who have created this World from the things we believe and the things we repeat over and over again and think over and over again about... It is because God has created us allowing us the freedom to Choose. So, if we keep showing to the Universe (or God) that we like to crib and that we like not to like this person or that we are more comfortable talking about things we do not have in life, the Universe makes that possible. By now, you should have understood that in this journey ?

God knows everything(Omniscience) – There is nothing that we need to tell God. He or She knows everything that was, is and will ever be. Then do we need to be anxious or worry about what happens in our life? Do we need to specifically tell God about what we need, how we need and when we need things? Or wouldn't it be better to Surrender to God?

(I have used 'God' as a representation of the Divine. It can be Goddess or Guru or Spirit or the Universe...)

Detachment

But before that, we will need to learn to detach from our attachments in life.

What are the attachments in life?

All the things that our ego owns ?

Which means everything in life that we Chose as our own. These can also be our family, our home, our region of the country, our language, our religion, our dialect, our enemies, our pet peeves, all of them. If we feel we cannot survive without something, that is our attachment. These include the things which we normally connect to and also the things which give us the will to survive which may not necessarily be 'good things'. For example, if you are taking decision based on the way it will harbour the animosity you have always had to your enemies, your enemies are your deep attachment. Even when you outwardly say, 'no they don't matter'.

So, to detach from these, how do you move away from them?

So, you don't have to move away. It is the feeling of Accepting them as being whoever they are and giving them the freedom to be without engaging in thoughts about them. Sounds so much like Love right? Yes, it is! It is allowing them space to be, not being affected by what happens to them knowing that too is being done by the Divine and letting go of all thoughts about them.

Does this mean to keep away from the things you have been told do not work for your betterment like liquor, smoking, etc? No. Detachment is the ability to be with it, even do it if you want to, knowing very well that you can live away from it and not miss it at all. That is the True end of it.

The 'keeping away' is pushing the urge under the carpet. It will remain there for as long as we keep our mind away from it. The minute you look at it, it breaks lose and comes through.

The cases of sexual exploitation by religious who preach against it, addictions of people who are leading anti-alcoholism measures etc are coming from this very same aspect of trying to push it under the carpet. True detachment occurs only when people are able to look at the person or thing they were attached to in the eye and feel nothing at all for it. Everything beyond is a Choice.

And how do we get to this state?

Observe your thoughts. Again, Observation does not mean to be engaged to the thoughts as they happen. Just Witness the thoughts as they move along the canvas of your mind. Label them. "Ah, there is a thought on my looks... there is one on my enemy... there is one on being unsuccessful... there is one on being super successful..."

As we continue to Observe, the thoughts diminish. And soon you will be able to Observe the blank spaces in between thoughts.

The nothingness...

Now just Observe your breath...

Surrender

Look back at your life. Is everything happening as you planned it? Are you satisfied with life? Perhaps you are, perhaps you are not... For those who are, are you a worrier or a doer? For those are not, does your worrying or your cribbing help you in anyway?

What if we just Accepted the above statements about God and just Surrendered all of it to Him or Her (yes people, God or Goddess) and just Accepted that every thought that flows through you is from God and every action is from God, everything that you are experiencing is God experiencing what He or She wants to experience and leave it at that?

And then watch the magic! If the magic is taking time and you are still faced with problems, watch your thoughts. Are they Trusting the Divine at all times? Trust and Surrender again.

Yes, thoughts will come which question your process, which question Surrender, which question God, which question non-doing and many more questions. Surrender them all again to the Divine.

Now, sit back and enjoy the magic!

I am God!

Yes, I just said it. Phew! ?

Now that does not mean I am the Chosen one. We all are. You are the form of the Divine experiencing exactly what you Chose to experience in this moment.

Pause, read that again. If you have understood that the Divine is Omnipotent, Omnipresent and Omniscient, isn't it you as well? Isn't it who is thinking reading this? Isn't it True?

It is.

Yes, it just is.

We are the versions of the Divine who are ignorant that we are Divine. Everything around us is also Divine. The air between us... The space between the air molecules... The ground beneath us... The trees around us... The filth around us... The dead bodies around us... The birds around us... All of it...

We are only taking these various forms to satisfy the curiosity in ourselves to understand 'how does this feel like'. And when we are satisfied or when we are done with one round in it, we Choose to move on. This Choosing may not be at the level of your thinking (it can be as well). It is at the level of the higher Consciousness within you (which some of you who have reached till here may already be experiencing).

To reach this higher level of Consciousness regularly and later become one with it, let the ego die out and focussing on meditating on the Sahasrara.

Letting the ego die

Everything that has prevented the merger of the kundalini with the Sahasrara is the ego. It raises its head at all points reminding we are still in the stage of separation from the Divine.

And here let me make it clear, the ego is not only the 'bad thoughts' you may have. The ego is also the so called 'good' but exclusive thoughts that we have.

We have learnt to clear all the aspects of the negative ego till now. What about the positive ego? What about the part of you that says 'I have only done good in this World so I deserve happiness' or 'I am practicing all that is Spiritual as told to me by the Guru, so I am Spiritual. I am special'.

Thoughts of separateness from the others and hence the Divine hold us right where we are. And until we let go of this and look at the Wisdom in its all roundedness, we will still justify the delay in the merging with the Sahasrara as 'it is not yet time for me' or 'the Divine is still not yet ready to merge' ?

Letting go of the ego means letting go of all the egoistic attachments in the Spiritual space as well. It involves letting go of any feelings of superiority that we may feel towards others because of our Spiritual connection, our path, our Guru, our concepts of the Divine and merging it in to the whole.

Think of the generations of people and the large populations of people who have resided on this Earth without being touched by the knowledge of your God or Goddess. Are they not children of the same Divine?

Let go... You are Truly not special in anyway... You are only as special as the Divine itself.

The Divine merging

When the 'I' of the ego leaves us, the merging automatically occurs. The merging is the most amazing process which cannot be described without the ego coming in.

The merging is a merging of the eager and expectant human form with the ever-ready and expectant Divine form. The minute the two dimensions merge, there is a combined explosion of all the senses within and outside the body. What happens then can only be described as Blissful! The experience is of us being one with the Universe...

The state stays for as long as we remain away from our ego. When the ego creeps in, it dissipates.

Meditation on the Sahasrara

Sit down cross legged and with an erect spine in a quiet and comfortable area. Take your attention to those parts of your body which are calling out to you. Give them your full attention. Tell them "I am with you" and mean it. Wait till all of them relax.

Now move your attention to your breath. Observe the breath as it moves into your nostril, into your body, into your lungs and Observe the receding breath as it leaves your lungs, leaves the nasal passages and moves out of your body. Observe this for a few cycles.

Now take your awareness along the spine and up through the chakras and the Sushumna nadi and out of your body a few inches above your head. Enter the Sahasrara space.

Feel yourself enveloped with Loving presence of your own higher self. Allow your awareness to leak out of your edges and borders of what you think is the end of you. Allow the awareness to slowly spread out into what you think or feel is the space of the Higher self.

Breathe...

Just be in that space for as long as you want...

When you feel complete, thank your Higher self and allow your awareness to slowly come back into your body into this space and time.

Rub your palms and place them over your eyes. Gently open your eyes.

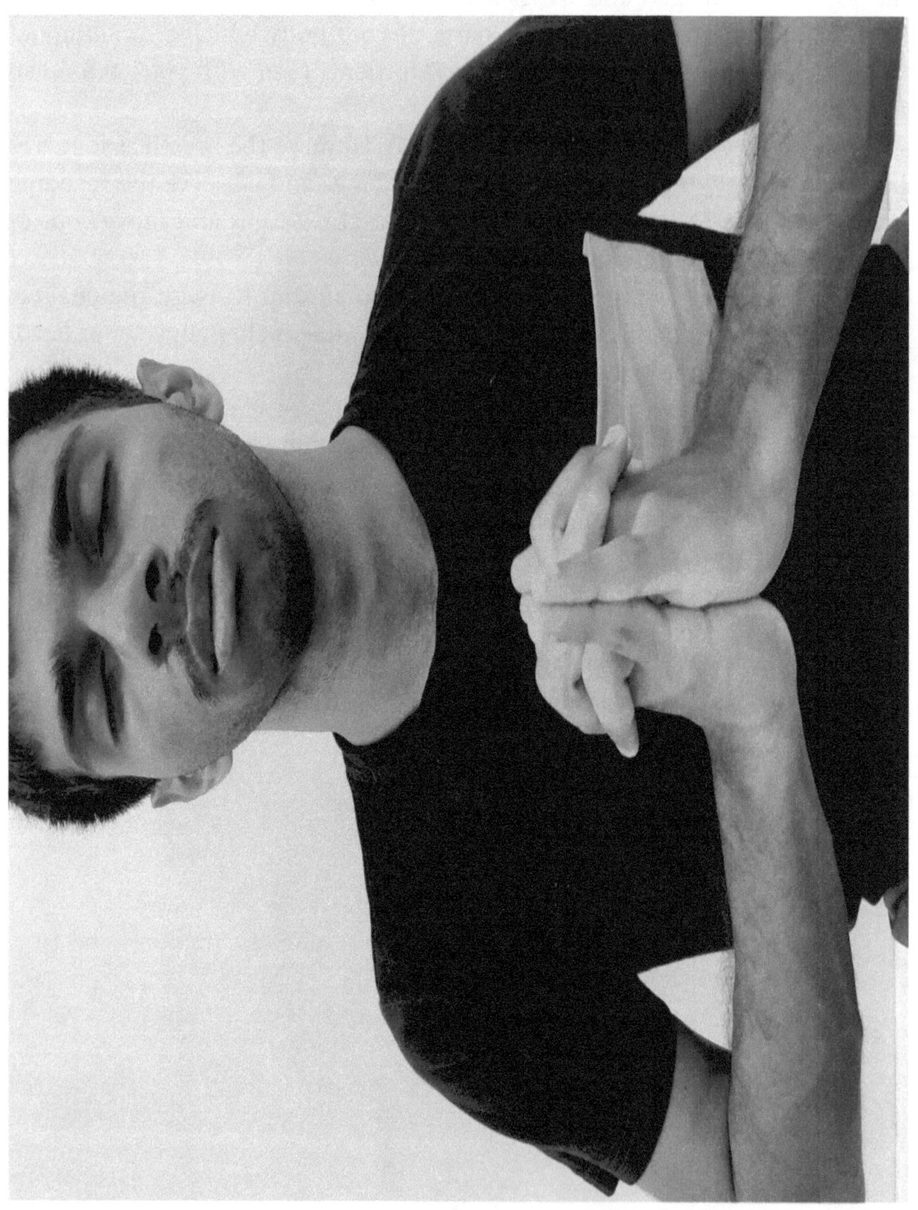

Fig 16: The hand position (mudra) for the Crown Chakra

Now!

What was the time when you were in touch with your Higher self? Where were you? Were there any thoughts or visions about the past or the future? If so, where did they seem to happen?

In the here... In the now!

We humans have been used to the linear mode of seeing life as a beginning when we are born and an end when we die. Perhaps it is not so. Perhaps there is a reality where every version of you in the present life and so called past and future lives are living in parallel in the now! And that is what the Higher self shows you.

The potent Power of change is in the now!

The energy of the Divine is with you in the now!

The Divine as we know it is not different from you in the now!

You are Eternal in the now!

If you learn to make this connection with the Higher self in the now, you can manifest anything! You are the Divine... You are the centre of the Universe...

Oneness

You may want to manifest those things you have always wanted to, like the car with the top down and of the latest make, the home on the beach, the dream job, the heart throb in your life, but you don't feel like doing it when you are one with the Higher self... Why is that?

You are also in the space of being one with everything that is. You realise that it is you only which is the road beneath the tracks, you are the vehicle on it, you are the driver, you are the wind, you are the destination, you are the experience. And when you realise this, it does not really matter!

You are all the people around you, you are their dreams, their despair, the ambition, the mirth, the introspection, all of it... You are everything. You are me!

While this feeling is so beautiful, you realise you would not want to alter it at all! Yes, you wouldn't want to alter the prevailing situation in the whole wide world! Because you are aware how it is all going to be. You would never want to change that experience for all the parts of you!

As you regularly build up this Oneness feeling within you, you can even exude a space where anyone who wishes anything can just come near you and think it and it shall be done. This is the secret behind all the manifestations around the masters and gurus.

Let's understand this Oneness better. This is a feeling which is all Accepting. It is completely non-judgemental. It exhudes Love. It is One!

What about life after the Oneness experience?

Life is never the same again – Never!

We begin to Trust and Accept every place as beautiful in it's own natural way...

We begin to Accept every person around us in their own natural way...

We begin to understand that just like us, everything has the potential to change into anything at any given point in time – Nothing and everything

We begin to become Love and exude it from wherever we are...

We begin to orient ourselves to the ultimate situation in any circumstance...

We stop judging people... We know that everything we see are just the polarities in our mind...

We begin to live the Oneness Truth...

The Eternal self

The Eternal Self feeling grows into you as you practice the chants and the practices listed here. The Truth begins to percolate into you that you are more than just this body – you have experienced life with and without illnesses, you have experienced life without the pleasures of the body and the hurts. These are all transient. Who is the one beyond these experiences within you?

The Truth begins to percolate within you that you are not these emotions as well. You realise you are the same being within who experiences Joy and then sorrow and then frustration and then exhilaration and you Observe yourself having felt differently in all of them. So, what is the core you?

The Truth percolates within you that you are neither the numerous thoughts that have taken over your mind at various times. The thoughts of ambition, the thoughts of desperation, the thoughts of jealousy, the thoughts of motivation all just move past the canvas of your mind. So, what is the True you beneath all of this?

And that is the Eternal self! Though explained so simply, it is when you start Observing the characteristics of this permanent self that you begin to settle into it. You become comfortable. You reach Peace...

Wisdom of the Sahasrara chakra

1. We are the Divine
2. Read 1. again ?

The Divine life begins...

www.ingramcontent.com/pod-product-compliance
Lightning Source LLC
Chambersburg PA
CBHW031305130726
47988CB00007B/2735